# Talking Stick 27

# New Arrangements

The Talking Stick
Volume 27

A publication of the
Jackpine Writers' Bloc, Inc.
Menahga, Minnesota

The Talking Stick Volume 27

© Copyright 2018 Jackpine Writers' Bloc, Inc.
Menahga, Minnesota
Printed in the United States of America
All rights reserved by the authors.
ISBN # 978-1-928690-37-5.

www.thetalkingstick.com
www.jackpinewriters.com
Send correspondence to sharrick1@wcta.net or
Jackpine Writers' Bloc, Inc., 13320 149th Avenue,
Menahga, Minnesota 56464.

Managing Editors: Sharon Harris, Tarah L. Wolff
Copy Editors: Sharon Harris, Niomi Rohn Phillips, Marilyn D. Wolff
Layout, Production and Cover Design: Tarah L. Wolff
Editorial Board: Marlys Guimaraes, Sharon Harris, Mike Lein,
    Ryan Neely, Tarah L. Wolff
Judges: Niomi Rohn Phillips and Scott Stewart
Cover Photograph: Kevin Zepper

## List of Contributors

| | |
|---|---|
| Luke Anderson | 132, 141 |
| Lina Belar | 63, 118 |
| James Bettendorf | 102 |
| Nicole Borg | 28, 66 |
| Janice Larson Braun | 88, 146 |
| | |
| Tim J. Brennan | 78, 94 |
| Sue Bruns | 2, 39, 110 |
| Marc Burgett | 154 |
| Julie Chattopadhyay | 84 |
| Sharon Chmielarz | 182 |
| | |
| Jan Chronister | 165 |
| Chet Corey | 29 |
| Frances Ann Crowley | 8, 53 |
| Norita Dittberner-Jax | 80 |
| Charmaine Pappas Donovan | 48 |
| | |
| Neil Dyer | 55 |
| Larry Ellingson | 25 |
| Jeanne Emrich | 70 |
| Jeanne Everhart | 81, 135 |
| Edis Flowerday | 85 |
| | |
| Cindy Fox | 126, 147, 155 |
| Shelley Getten | 131 |
| Katie Gilbertson | 171 |
| Georgia A. Greeley | 77, 124, 158 |
| Marlys Guimaraes | 95, 166 |

## List of Contributors

| | |
|---|---|
| Carla Hagen | 46 |
| Laura L. Hansen | 160, 178 |
| JJ Harrigan | 99 |
| Sharon Harris | 15, 33, 106 |
| Audrey Kletscher Helbling | 123 |
| | |
| Jennifer Hernandez | 11, 24, 31 |
| John Herold | 18 |
| Dennis Herschbach | 9, 38 |
| Angela Hunt | 146 |
| Harrison Hurd | 30, 113 |
| | |
| Jim Jasken | 98 |
| Christina Joyce | 61 |
| Meridel Kahl | 17, 149 |
| James Robert Kane | 4 |
| Paisley Kauffmann | 151 |
| | |
| Vicky A. King | 1 |
| Norma Thorstad Knapp | 43, 107 |
| Sue Kral | 134 |
| Kim A. Larson | 71, 122 |
| Kristin Laurel | 181 |
| | |
| Mike Lein | 139 |
| Dawn Loeffler | 32, 40, 111 |
| Tenlee Lund | 67, 163 |
| J. Mackenzie | 49 |
| Cheyenne Marco | 129 |

## List of Contributors

| | |
|---|---|
| Alice Marks | 105 |
| Margaret M. Marty | 69 |
| Michael McCormick | 16 |
| Susan McMillan | 79, 97 |
| Michele Micklewright | 125 |
| | |
| Michael Kiesow Moore | 64 |
| Marsh Muirhead | 159, 167 |
| Marcia Neely | 161 |
| Ryan M. Neely | 41, 91, 115 |
| L. E. Newsom | 7 |
| | |
| Joni Norby | 109 |
| David Eric Northington | 138 |
| Vincent O'Connor | 34 |
| Andrew O'Kelley | 103 |
| Ronald J. Palmer | 117 |
| | |
| Yvonne Pearson | 14 |
| Susan Perala-Dewey | 74 |
| Niomi Rohn Phillips | 19, 51, 179 |
| Deborah Rasmussen | 23 |
| Kate Ritger | 150, 169 |
| | |
| Kit Rohrbach | 137, 142 |
| Lane Rosenthal | 164 |
| Joy Saethre | 75 |
| Deb Schlueter | 119 |
| Jean Scoon | 56, 143 |

## List of Contributors

| | |
|---|---|
| Richard Fenton Sederstrom | 60, 177 |
| Stephen Sinicrope | 47 |
| Beth Spencer | 27, 90 |
| Peter Stein | 52 |
| Doris Lueth Stengel | 174 |
| | |
| Scott Stewart | 157 |
| Marlene Mattila Stoehr | 35, 128 |
| Bernadette Hondl Thomasy | 127 |
| Peggy Trojan | 130 |
| Donna Uphus | 175 |
| | |
| Beth L. Voigt | 57 |
| Susan Niemela Vollmer | 37 |
| Marg Walker | 89, 112 |
| Elizabeth Weir | 59 |
| Ben Westlie | 65 |
| | |
| Cheryl Weibye Wilke | 22 |
| Tarah L. Wolff | 133 |
| Cathy Wood | 168 |

## Co-Editor's Note – Sharon Harris

Editor's Choice: "This New Arrangement" (p.89)
by Marg Walker

My choice for favorite writing this year is: "This New Arrangement" by Marg Walker on Page 89. This poem intrigued many of us from the beginning. I have been in this place. I have been in a relationship and lived in a house as a couple. Then we were not together and I scarcely even knew how it happened. We managed to stay close and still converse, still see each other—the love was still there—but it wasn't the same. A new person could come into the equation and I would be completely outside. Things did move and change and I had no say in their movement or their changing. I felt like I was there but not there. This poem says so much in a few suggestive descriptions, a quiet heartbreak, a silent yearning—a missing of what is gone and cannot exist again.

It is intriguing each year that we can usually see themes appearing as we read the submissions. One year the words "Black and White" were mentioned in many stories and that became the subtitle of the book. Some years most stories seem to center on death or on going home or on things that happened in the past. Sometimes our subtitle comes from lines in some of the poems or stories. Ideally, the subtitle reflects both the cover and the submissions. This year we seemed to mainly have stories about dead pets but we couldn't use that. Then we noticed that we had many break-ups and losses and changes in relationships. We also had many mentions of cows and old barns and things changing. So we focused on endings and changes and new arrangements and thus the subtitle *New Arrangements*.

I often use this space in my Editor's Note to remind writers how our procedures work each year. Last year and this year, we tried something a little different, asking for shorter submissions. Even though we had that slight change, we still want to continue our quest to publish Minnesota writers or those with a strong connection to Minnesota. We like some stories with a Northwoods flavor and we like to create a book with some heartwarming but still with sometimes a lesson-to-learn-type of writing. After our March 1 deadline, then we have five of our members form as the Editorial Board to read all the submissions and then choose the poems and stories that we want in the book. They also choose the top ones for honorable mention and possible prizes. Those of us on the Board of Directors or our Editorial Board are not eligible for the prizes. Then we remove the names from those top choices and we have an impartial judge choose the first and second place for the prize money in each genre. These judges have also been gracious enough to supply some helpful comments and suggestions on those top submissions. This year, we also tried another new item. We decided to give a Humor prize for the most humorous writing from any of the three genres.

We hope you all enjoyed the challenge of writing shorter, more concise submissions as much as we did. We would love to hear from you, the submitters, regarding whether you like the shorter submission requirements or not.

www.sharonharrispoetry.com

## Co-Editor's Note – Tarah L. Wolff
Editor's Choice: "Family Traditions" (p.179)
by Niomi Rohn Phillips

There were many poems and stories this year that rang true for our chosen subtitle of *New Arrangements*. From divorce to death, to the inevitable changes of life like the family farm slipping away to the past. They all spoke true to my own situation during this last long, endless winter.

I live in my grandparents' old farmhouse and every day, when I drive home, I ask my one-hundred-year-old barn to keep standing even as she quietly slips closer to the earth. There will someday be the inevitable new arrangement of my adjusting to the barn no longer being in my yard. I have already begun plans to replace trees that my grandparents removed, to add privacy and wind breaks but, mostly, to add substance to a yard that will be tragically empty when that day comes.

My editor's choice will not surprise anyone who is close to me as I have become known now as Grandma's House DIY. I am approaching the dream of most writers: to one day be able to write for a living and, with my blog about my Grandma's house, that dream is slowly becoming my reality. In Niomi's wonderful piece she beautifully describes a family gathering in another culture, proving that grandmothers carry the same love and worry in every corner of the world.

My new arrangement this year was a divorce that helped prove to me, once and for all, that yes, the good things end but it also means the bad do, too. Some endings are wonderful changes to be celebrated. I remind myself of this when I look at my old barn. Even as we grieve the loss of some things, many times it means the opening of a place for new and wonderful things. New experiences, new chances and fantastic new arrangements.

www.grandmashousediy.com

## First Place

### Poetry – "Pain"
### Vicky A. King (p.1)

Vicky A. King was born and raised in southern Minnesota. She was part of a poetry project assembling submissions from the area into small bound books called *The Millpond Journal*, a rewarding venture to unmask "closet poets." She has been published in *Austin Living Magazine*, *Poetic Strokes*, and *Sidewalks*.

### Creative Nonfiction – "The Magician"
### Sue Bruns (p.2)

Sue Bruns retired from Bemidji High School in 2010 to devote time to her lifelong passion of writing. She writes a monthly column and historical articles for *The Bemidji Pioneer*, dabbles in various genres, and enjoys them all. She lives on Lake Plantagenet with her husband and two adopted dogs.

### Fiction – "What My Heart Knows"
### James Robert Kane (p.4)

James Robert Kane writes fiction from flash length to novels. He has published four e-books, two now in print version, and his work has appeared in several anthologies and an online magazine. He attends two writers' groups and is currently working to help veterans heal through writing. He is retired and lives in Chaska, Minnesota.

### Humor – "Practical Gifts"
### L. E. Newsom (p.7)

L. E. Newsom is an emerging writer. She has kept journals for many years and would like to transform them into writings that people would enjoy reading. She is taking classes at the Loft in Minneapolis to help her achieve her goal.

New Arrangements

## Second Place

Poetry – "In His Wake"
Frances Ann Crowley (p.8)

Creative Nonfiction – "Under the Nighttime Sky"
Dennis Herschbach (p.9)

Fiction – "Our Mother's Tattoo"
Jennifer Hernandez (p.11)

## Honorable Mention

**Poetry**
"Alzscape Reflection" – Jim Jasken (p.98)
"Vengeance of the Wind" – Alice Marks (p.105)
"Bright Room with Linoleum Floor, 1993" – Marg Walker (p.112)

**Creative Nonfiction**
"The Behavior Plan" – Marlene Mattila Stoehr (p.35)
"Nothing to Fight For" – Norma Thorstad Knapp (p.107)
"In Memoriam" – Tenlee Lund (p.163)

**Fiction**
"Moving On" – Jean Scoon (p.143)
"Haunted" – Jeanne Everhart (p.81)
"Parting Shots" – Audrey Kletscher Helbling (p.123)

**Humor (any genre)**
Poetry – "That Suit" – Jean Scoon (p.56)
Poetry – "Looking Over My Shoulder" – Harrison Hurd (p.30)
Creative Nonfiction – "Girlfriend" – Harrison Hurd (p.113)
Fiction – "My Retirement Plan" – Katie Gilbertson (p.171)

# New Arrangements

Vicky A. King – Poetry – First Place

# Pain

Sometimes when words
have fallen away
When the bruised apple lies
still under the boughs
too damaged to speak
She stands
flour to her elbows
punching down the dough
until it weeps
Seas cresting in her eyes
red lips trembling
hands too focused to shake
Sometimes in such silence
her propped-open screen door
was the only way
that she could breathe

Sue Bruns – Creative Nonfiction – First Place

# The Magician

He'd been sent to my office—again. The California kid with the chip on his shoulder. His attitude could find its way under my skin, but I wouldn't let that happen today.

"Tell me what happened?" I asked him. I'd already heard the accusation, but I'd listen to his version first. He skipped the part about being caught with his girlfriend in a bathroom stall after school and went straight for the jugular of the hall monitor: "She hates me. She's always trying to get me in trouble." More words, but something else—not about the hall monitor or me or about getting caught. Just anger.

I sat behind my desk, listening—not to the words, but to that anger and, when he took a breath, I looked directly at him and said, with genuine concern, "What has made you such an angry person?"

He was incredulous at first. Words didn't come, but something neither of us expected: tears. They fell down his California-tanned face, releasing the anger. And when he found his voice, he spoke of a mother who had better things to do than raise a son, so she sent him to live in freezing Minnesota in the middle of February—to live with a father he barely knew.

We concluded our business and, as he left my office, I thought, "That was a magical question."

A few days later a ninth-grade girl was sent to my office—smoking in the locker room. Her fists were clenched with rage. I let her talk, and her fists grew tighter. She danced around the story with lies and excuses, but something else, too. And when she paused, I looked into her troubled eyes and heard myself wonder aloud, "What has made you such an angry person?"

And the reaction surprised us both. Tears fell, spilling her pent-up anger, releasing a flood of injustices.

When she left my office, I stepped out to my secretary's desk. "I've found the magic question," I told her, and I returned to my office to contemplate my new-found power.

Later that week a transfer student was sent to my office. She'd threatened to beat up another girl. Nothing in her words or demeanor led me to believe she wouldn't follow through on the threat. There must be more to this story, I thought, so I let her talk, not even interrupting the fog of obscenities that spewed from her mouth. Finally, I raised my hand in a "halt" gesture to interrupt the flow of her language. I looked her in the eyes, asked the magic question: "What has made you such an angry person?" and waited for the reaction.

She paused long enough to inhale, leaned across my desk until our faces were just inches apart and said, "What the fuck do you care?"

I wrote up the suspension, sent her home, and delivered the report to my secretary.

"Two out of three ain't bad," she said.

James Robert Kane – Fiction – First Place
# What My Heart Knows

The girl is in trouble.

One long look tells me this.

Thumb out for a hitch, she seems disturbingly detached as she leans forward against the weight of a large backpack. Expressionless face. Vacant eyes. Inanimate.

Used up.

Dead girl standing.

And I pass her by.

I feel guilty about that but I am in no mood to be a good Samaritan, motherly instincts notwithstanding. I am still decompressing from a stressful drive through disorienting fog masking Highway 61 between Castle Danger and Lutsen. Enough drama for one day and a lousy start to a much-needed extended vacation up on the Gunflint Trail. I desperately need cleansing sauna sweats, tranquil kayaking, and peaceful hikes. Portals to healing, I hope. From grief. My husband understands. He sent me.

And I am almost there, just a mile from my turnoff at Grand Marais. That's another reason I don't stop. She probably wants a longer lift. Plus, lots of other cars are on the road. Somebody else will help.

I cling to these excuses as she gets smaller and smaller in the rearview mirror.

And disappears.

Yet I cannot unsee her.

I do a U-turn at the Angry Trout.

Unfocused green eyes flick briefly across me as I pull up close. I cautiously lower the front passenger side window partway and loudly ask, "You okay?"

She turns and says into the opening, "Know where a hospital is?"

I am digging for my phone, wondering why she doesn't seem to have one, when I hear her tug the rear passenger side door open. I must have unlocked it feeling for the window switch.

"Hey," I protest, but she seems not to hear. She tosses her stuff onto the back seat and piles in after it, half reclining against her pack, one arm dangling and legs long and loose, a pose of capitulation. I get out and scurry to the still-open door. She is filthy. So is her gear. Obviously on the road awhile. No makeup. Shoulder-length, dull brown hair in disarray. Nails unpainted and ragged. And she doesn't seem concerned about surrendering herself to a stranger.

She also doesn't seem like much of a threat.

I do a search instead of calling 911. Grand Marais has a hospital. I close the door gently against her feet.

Her lethargy persists on the way but as we arrive, she sees a police car parked at the emergency entrance and instantly becomes energized.

"Don't stop!"

"Why?"

"Just go!" Her eyes turn wild and frantic and dangerous-looking and I fear I might get stabbed if I stop, so I accelerate away. We turn off into the downtown and I drive slowly, repeatedly cruising the compact circuit, wondering what to do with her. She has become quiet again, and when I peek over the bucket seats she is rag-doll limp, sunk into her gear. *Passed out?* I wonder. *Or worse?*

I pull to the curb near the Blue Water Cafe, turn in my seat and gently shake her shoulder. No response. Check for a pulse. Not dead. Yet.

I race back to the hospital and pull up behind the

squad car we fled. The cops gently extract her and her gear.

Her eyes open as they strap her onto the gurney.

She sees the officers. Looks angrily into my forty-year-old eyes. "You bitch!"

I'm sad for her but mostly relieved as I watch them wheel her away. That feeling evaporates as an officer taking one more look for gear in my back seat finds a baggie half full of . . .

"Weed," he announces loudly.

Everything turns out all right for me at the police station. Don't know about the girl. I check back and learn that she slipped out of the hospital and disappeared. She is very much present inside me though and, as I sit on my cabin deck, I cannot stop wondering about the how and why of her.

This much I know for sure: Tomorrow I am going to pause this vacation and go look for her.

My brain says this makes no sense. *You cannot possibly rescue her*, it argues. *And it will not bring back your daughter, murdered at college one year ago.*

My brain is probably right.

But it knows nothing about what is going on in my heart.

New Arrangements

L. E. Newsom – Creative Nonfiction – First Place Humor

# Practical Gifts

I prefer to give a practical gift when a gift-giving occasion arises. Sometimes that can be very challenging. If I had any grandkids, I would be the Grandma who gave them clothes and school supplies rather than video games or Pokémon cards.

I take that approach with John as well. Just before Valentine's Day as I was cruising the Walmart, I came across one of those blanket kits comprised of two pieces of fleece and you tie the edges together to make it. The best part was the picture on it was Wonder Woman. Early in our relationship John had informed me that we were history when Wonder Woman or Stevie Nicks appeared on our doorstep and asked him to come out and play. So, I thought he might like to cuddle with Wonder Women while he continued to wait for any real appearances.

Practicality can include side benefits, too. For Christmas, I had given him a multicolored five-pack of knit boxers. It had taken me quite a while to choose the exact package as I wanted one with four dark colors and one red pair. I thought having one red pair would assist in clear communication for us. When he was interested in some action he was to be sporting the red pair. When I saw him in the red pair I would know I was to be in the mood. I explained all this as he was opening the gift.

Several days passed and he had broken in all the dark pairs. The red pair was still crisp and new and at the bottom of the dresser drawer. And so, I waited. Time passed quickly as days turned into weeks and weeks into months. Long about the summer solstice, I decided I needed to take some further steps to trigger the desired outcome. On the night before an early shift when I knew he would blindly reach into the underwear drawer and put on what he found, I removed all the dark pairs, leaving only the red pair.

He went to work commando that day.

Frances Ann Crowley – Poetry – Second Place

# In His Wake

It is Winter Solstice Eve.
Pines gift the air.
Raspberry thorns glisten and display their snags
of grocery sack and yellowed newspaper.
The yard light's flicker exposes a middle-aged Ford,
a ceremony of sparrows under the empty feeder,
and a graying mailbox—
dented and tilted by last year's plow.
Pale corn stubble pokes through snow cover.
A grand and grave oak stands in the middle
of the field. Gnarly fingers beckon.

Down at Lucky's, old-timers feed the jukebox
and clink their glasses. Imprints of coffin
handles linger on their palms.

Dennis Herschbach – Creative Nonfiction – Second Place

# Under the Nighttime Sky

The leather cover of the scrapbook was scuffed, its corners worn. Inside, pasted to the first yellowed page was the picture of a soldier with the caption "Eighteen-year-old Carl Plath has completed basic and infantry training in Florida."

I turned the pages: a letter from the soldier to his mother telling her the army wasn't all that bad; a note saying he'd be boarding a ship soon but couldn't divulge its destination; another letter with words blacked out; one with a military postmark of June, 1944.

*Dear Ma, Something big is happening, I can't tell you what, but I won't be able to write for a while. Don't worry. I'm okay. Someday, I'll tell you all about it.*

The next entry held an ominous message sent in October, 1944, from the government: Carl was a prisoner of war and was held in Stalag 2B in Poland. What followed were a few letters via the Red Cross telling his mother to not worry. Pasted alone was a message from the government declaring Carl was being marched over four hundred miles from Poland to someplace near Berlin. On the next page was written this prayer:

*Please God, give my son strength, and I know what little food they give him. I know God, you can take a crust of bread and supply a million, so please God, be with him when the way is too long, the body too weary, and food too meager. God, make it enough to give him strength, give him courage to make the way shorter and, no matter how weary he is, walk beside him.*

There was no other entry in the book until April, 1945. It was a form statement with blanks filled in: the date, place, and name of her soldier. The message was a copy from Germany listing where Carl was being held.

There was nothing in the scrapbook of how he was taken prisoner along with his platoon, no record of an SS officer holding a trial where the prisoners were convicted in the field of war crimes; no account of the same officer going down the line, executing them. No one reading the scrapbook would hear the Allied fighter plane dive from the sky on a strafing run, or see the survivors piled into a truck and carted away. No one would know of the interrogations or the four-hundred-mile forced march during the winter to just outside Berlin. The beatings, the starvation, the disease—none of these accounts could be in the book. Only the last entry written on Red Cross stationary and dated April, 1945:

*Dear Ma, I'm writing to let you know that I'm okay, so don't worry. They treat me well, and someday I'll be able to come home. And Ma, tonight go out and look at the stars. They are the same stars I see from here. Love, your son, Carl.*

Jennifer Hernandez – Fiction – Second Place

## Our Mother's Tattoo

Our mother had a tattoo. We never knew until after she died. She was an intensely private person, always locked the door of the bathroom, even when we were young. I remember the shock of staying at my cousin's house as a girl, the way her mom—my father's sister—would stand in front of the bathroom mirror putting on her make-up, wearing nothing but a bra and panties, the door wide open, carrying on a full conversation with us all the while. At our house, we had trouble getting my mother to carry on a conversation when we were all at the dinner table fully clothed.

She loved us. There was no question of that. She showed her love in a million unspoken ways from the special treats she would include in our lunchboxes—both homemade baked goods and store-bought "junk" purchased behind our father's back—to the lavender sachets she would tuck into our dresser drawers so that our T-shirts would smell "like the French countryside." She just wasn't a big conversationalist.

The funeral director was the one who alerted us to the existence of the tattoo. He had prepared her body for the viewing. She lay in the casket in the navy blue long-sleeved silk dress that we had selected from her closet, the one with a flowy skirt just past the knee.

He asked us, "Who is Jacob?"

My sister Elizabeth gave me a pained look, already concerned that the funeral director was not quite all there. "Jacob?" she intoned. "What Jacob?"

"The Jacob in the tattoo," he replied, tucking a wisp

of gray hair behind my mother's ear.

Elizabeth and I exchanged glances. "What tattoo?" she said.

"Your mother's tattoo."

Our protestations ended when he gently moved aside the silky fabric of her bodice to reveal the tattoo just above her left breast, a small red heart with the name *Jacob* inside.

Not knowing much about tattoos, it was difficult for us to guess how long ago she had gotten this one. Her skin was thin and wrinkled with age, but the name in the tattoo was clear. We didn't know a Jacob.

Was Jacob a secret gentleman friend? But why would she keep him a secret? Our parents had been divorced for over twenty years. We would have been thrilled for her to have found new love. Our dad had remarried within two years of their divorce, and our mother's relative isolation filled us with a heavy sense of obligation.

Maybe Jacob was married to someone else, and our mother's torrid love affair with him had to remain a secret.

Maybe Jacob was her first love, before Dad entered the picture. Maybe he was a soldier in Vietnam and never made it back. Maybe her unresolved feelings over having lost him poisoned her relationship with our father and even kept her from finding someone new after they split up.

Maybe we had a brother, the one we had always wanted. Maybe Jacob was conceived before our mother was married. Maybe she was spirited off to a home for unwed mothers, her baby taken before she was even allowed to hold him. Maybe a sympathetic nun let slip that the baby was a boy, and our mother named him Jacob. Maybe Jacob came later, between my sister and I, or after. Or maybe he was stillborn and never spoken of again.

We couldn't ask our dad or, rather, we could ask him, as his ashes sat in a brass urn on my fireplace mantel, but we weren't likely to get a satisfactory response.

We were half-hoping that the mysterious Jacob would show up at the visitation or funeral and introduce himself, but no such luck. We even scoured the guest book. No Jacob.

I decided that the only thing I could do was to honor my mother's secret. So on the first anniversary of her death, I dragged Elizabeth with me to a tattoo parlor, and she held my hand while I got inked for the first (and last) time. A red heart with *Jacob* on my shoulder, because they say that's the least sensitive spot, and I hate needles.

When it's summer, and I can wear tank tops, I hope to be a walking billboard. I'm waiting for Jacob—whoever he is—to walk up and introduce himself. I'd really like to get to know my mother better.

Yvonne Pearson – Poetry
# Farm Summer

The day we mounted the horse—
    —*Princess*—
a tall and haunchy female,
I clung to your waist,
my own powerful female,
as Princess carried us
down the hill and into the pasture
to claim the cattle for milking.
She plunged into the shallow creek
and sank her fine-spun legs
deep in mud. Deep
in mud. My heart fluttered in fear
as the horse bucked and pulled.
Princess heaved herself, and us, free,
and we galloped up the hill
calling *Come boss,*
*come boss.* The reins lain lightly
against the agile neck
turned the horse left and right
through bristled pines
and the cattle lowed and then turned,
slowly as flowers closing for the night,
and lumbered toward the barn
where my uncle would lean his head
against each hot haunch in turn
and pull the milk, frothing white,
into pail after pail.

Sharon Harris – Creative Nonfiction
## Remembering Summers

In the summers when school was out, my sister and I would go to the library and each get seven books to read over the next week. We spent as much time as possible on our screened-in porch devouring those books. We would lie on our stomachs on our beds, a book propped in front of us, and float away to another world. Seven books and seven days and then we'd go back for more.

When we were not reading, we were doing chores in the barn: feeding the calves, giving them new bedding, or we'd be out in the woods bringing the cows home from the pasture for milking. I remember the heat shimmering in front of us as we walked, the insects around us, the swinging tails and swinging strides of the cows as we followed them home on well-worn paths through the hazel brush. Dust rose from their hooves and clung to our sweating bodies. The brush scratched our bare legs and the shrill whine of the grasshoppers filled the air around us. The insects leapt all over the place as the cows walked by, often landing on our legs or arms and clinging with a sticky feeling that we hated. Occasional walking sticks dropped on us from overhead branches and made us scream—they were stickier yet and had so many legs. Deer flies buzzed around our heads in endless, monotonous circles.

This was our whole world, our summers here on the farm—the summers that never seemed to end. The cows, the chores, the books—these were all we knew. We wanted to get those chores done and get back to our books on the cooler screened-in porch, maybe with a glass of Kool-Aid. There we could escape again to other worlds, an unending

number of places to go.
      Decades later, all those cows are long gone and even the paths through the brush are gone, grown over with grass and more brush—like they never were. But the books live on. The pages still turn, the words still call us and remind us there are other places to learn about.

Michael McCormick – Poetry

# Ex Poem

A poem was here once

I had it
twitching on a spiny hook

Pull it, hit it
trap it in a book

Sometimes a poem
is just a tire or a boot

Meridel Kahl – Poetry

# Legacy

A grandmother I never knew
was born in Germany
where geraniums
spill over balcony railings
cascade down walls
of white timber-frame homes
and glow from window boxes
high above narrow streets.

I've always wanted to find her
in some small thing
I do, to say *I got this from her*,
something more than
the color of my eyes or hair.

Each October I move
pots of geraniums inside.
I sweep orange-red petals
off the floor from December to March.
I like to think she did the same.

I bury my nose
in their peppery leaves
marvel at their blossoms
hanging like bright lanterns
and claim this
as her legacy to me.

John Herold - Poetry
## Brilliant Ideas

These spruce grow where they should never—
out of rock, immense rock,
with tiny cracks for toeholds.
And leaning into air above Lake Superior,
like a trapeze artist alone, unnoticed,
spreading both arms out to the world,
each tree knows
precarious fulfillment.

Hermits face sunrise across the lake,
spreading arms wide in acceptance.
Solitary, grounded in patience,
each one is somebody's far relative
keeping distant for his own good—
the silence and frugality
of practicing a discipline,
embracing a life free of triviality.

Say this immense rock is a brain
with ridges and huge lobes
rounded by wind and glacier,
for millions of years—
pondering, ruminating, and well rested.
In time the right intentions grow,
clinging from small cracks,
enriched with the soil of patience.

Niomi Rohn Phillips – Fiction
# Control-Alt-Delete

My sister Carol was only sixty when she died. I didn't get to the funeral, but our brother Vern said they had to custom-make a casket.

Mom blamed Carol's weight on her summer with Grandma and Grandpa on the farm. All that German food with cream on everything from cucumbers to peaches.

You should see her little girl photos—blonde curls, blue eyes, tiny nose. "What a cutie," old women muttered. You know how adults talk as if kids standing next to them are deaf.

Carol was a senior the year I got married. I spent a weekend nagging about bridesmaid dresses. "We have to take measurements. The dresses won't get here on time." Carol flounced out of the room in tears.

"Tonight's prom." Mom frowned at me. "Carol wasn't asked."

Sympathy flittered by, but I was focused on my wedding.

Carol didn't date in high school. Then she started sleeping around with guys from the Base and ended up pregnant. Enter Peter, loser husband.

One time Mom and Dad dropped in, and there wasn't even milk in the house for the baby. Peter was discharged, didn't have a job. Then he took off, left Carol with a baby and a two-year-old. First divorce in our family.

Mom wrote once that Carol was in the hospital with "nerves" and something about shock treatments. Mom and Dad had the kids. She never mentioned shock treatments again, and I didn't ask. Now there's no one to ask.

I googled "shock treatments." It's called Electroconvulsive Therapy now—ECT.

They attach electrodes to your temples. One blogger said she clenched her teeth, bit into the mouth guard. Her heart pounded. She thought she'd have a heart attack.

The treatments are for people who've tried every drug. It might prevent suicide. I don't know if Carol tried suicide. The treatments are like six to twelve shocks a day, three times a week. The electrodes on your head produce a seizure, like an epileptic.

I don't want to picture Carol on that table, her body jerking, gagging, eyes rolling back into her head. They say the seizure only lasts seconds. The patient doesn't remember a thing. Amnesia is one of the side effects. It's called "memory disturbance" now.

Some famous people had the treatment—Ernest Hemingway, Sylvia Plath. Some psychiatrists say the treatment is making a comeback. What they call e-currents "reboot the brain—like control/alt/delete when the computer locks."

Vern cleaned out Carol's house in Arkansas. I never got around to visiting her. Kept her "at arm's length," as Grandma advised if you wanted to avoid entanglements. I definitely didn't want entanglements in Carol's messy life.

In her forties she said she'd been diagnosed with fibromyalgia. I'd never heard of it. Another "woe is me" for Mom and Dad's benefit, I thought. Another time she said her boss was looking for an excuse to get rid of her. I was skeptical about that story, too.

I googled fibromyalgia. One blogger wrote that every muscle is on fire. She can't even walk. She can't sleep. *Life isn't worth living*, she says.

## New Arrangements

Carol's neighbors told Vern she hadn't left the house or worked in her gardens recently. The only visitor was UPS. They found her slumped over her computer.

Vern said Carol's closets and cupboards overflowed with stuff she'd ordered online—clothes, videos, romance novels, jewelry.

I picture her reading romance novels and watching videos all night, lumbering from bed to computer. The shades are drawn. She spends the day ordering things she always wanted—beautiful clothes, collectible dolls, jewelry. A stack of credit cards beside the computer. Maxed out at the end.

Vern arranged a service at Christians' Chapel. He was surprised at the turnout—all her neighbors with their kids and a dozen former colleagues, including several black women and a gay couple.

Turned out the story about losing her job was true. She challenged their "chauvinistic, homophobic pig supervisor," her friends said. They reminisced about her sense of humor and generous homemade gifts. Creative like our mom—a Martha Stewart. All news to me . . .

Vern photographed a "Stargazer" lily blooming above weeds in Carol's garden. Our grandmas had gardens. So did Mom and Dad. I didn't know Carol gardened.

Stargazer's my favorite lily. I didn't know it would grow in Arkansas like in Ohio. Way different Plant Zones. I wish I'd talked to Carol about it. "Too soon old, too late smart," Grandma always said.

Cheryl Weibye Wilke – Poetry

# Housewife

When I open the morning,
I search for the light
from a sunrise I can't see

until I go to my daughter's
window framed by thin cotton
of pink and blue blossoms

drawn by a Daughter who
lived there before her. One by
one, the house empties. He first

off to work to support
his family. Then she off to
high school to learn the ways

of saving bees and sustaining
her planet. A hive so much
larger than I'll ever know—A worker

who stayed behind to savor the sweet
from daybreak to flowers.

Deborah Rasmussen – Poetry

# Dark-Eyed Junco on Oberg Mountain

A slate-gray cowl marks
this tiny monk
at work
in his secluded monastery.

He pauses
to raise his wings in blessing
silent thanks
for the sanctuary
of autumn foliage

resettles them
into his modest robe
and resumes communion

with the body
with the blood
of mountain flora
unruffled

by a lone pilgrim
who stops
to savor avian ways
of worship.

Jennifer Hernandez – Poetry
## Marilyn's Tanning

Business was slow in the summer.
Who wants to bake in a pod when
you're in the middle of lake country?

The silver Quonset hut sits along
Highway 59, shimmering in the sunshine,
hand-lettered sign on the door with hours
and phone number, bold print so tourists
can see when they drive through town
on the way to their cabins.

Sometimes they stop at the gas station
or liquor store. Maybe visit one of three
Lutheran churches if they're feeling pious
or guilty. Burgers at Hillbillies Vittles
hit the spot (depending on who's working).

But Marilyn has three kids at home. Their dad
never made it back from WE Fest last year, so
she's taken matters into her own hands, earned
an online degree in massage therapy, amended
the Quonset sign in super-sized red letters.

She now books appointments solid
each summer weekend.

Larry Ellingson – Fiction

# Ana

I met Ana at the city pool. It was July and the concrete deck was hot and the air was thick with chlorine. Through the chain link fence, I saw two nuns ushering a group of children along, coaxing them into line. They marched toward the pool, all noise and energy, and Ana was in the midst of the gaggle. She stopped to speak to a sad-looking boy, putting her hand on his shoulder as she smiled into his face. The town kids in the pool saw them coming and climbed out of the water. Dripping, they stood inside the fence and watched as the migrant children passed. From my perch in the lifeguard chair I watched Ana as she walked past the fence, head raised, looking straight ahead.

The locals rolled up their towels and made for the exit as the Mexican kids poured out of the locker room, laughing and chattering. The pool filled with brown, splashing bodies, turning it into a tempestuous little sea. I saw that few of the children knew how to swim so I watched them closely. A few of the bolder ones clung to the side of the pool and moved hand over hand toward the deep end. I climbed down from my chair and told them that they needed to go back into the shallow area, but they only looked at me and smiled. Ana saw what I was trying to do and she came over and spoke to them in Spanish. Grudgingly they moved back to the shallow end of the pool. I turned to thank her and was immediately drawn into her brown face, into dark eyes above a rounded nose, into a gaze of hawk-like fierceness and intelligence.

Over the next few weeks the parade of children and nuns returned, and Ana was there, calming the rough child and encouraging the shy one. Each day I grew increasingly eager, even impatient to see her. I put two chairs on the deck so that we could sit side-by-side and watch the children in the pool while we talked. She said that she was helping the nuns to care for the children during the day while their parents worked in the fields. She told me about her home in Texas and how she missed her grandmother and the fried tortillas and pork she made like no other. She told me that her parents and her brother weeded and hoed the fields all day, bending their backs to the sky. When the nuns asked her father, he had reluctantly agreed to let her stay and help with the children. Ana was glad of this; it was better than an aching back, better than working in the heat and the dust in an endless row of beets.

    One day I asked Ana if she would meet me when I was finished at the pool and before she and the children were brought back to the farms. There was a park nearby and we walked along the river on top of an earthen dike that was supposed to keep the spring floodwaters in check. We held hands and walked and talked. I felt as if this was just one of an endless number of days we would have together. I asked her if we could meet again but she didn't reply; she just looked into my eyes and with a faint smile gently touched my arm.

    Of course we were noticed. It was a small town, everyone knew everyone. There were hard looks and moving lips. My parents folded their arms and said that it was over. When the Mexican kids came back to the pool, Ana was not with them. I looked for her at the school but the nuns sent me away. I went to the farm where they worked and was told that she was gone. One day the Mexican kids stopped coming to the pool. I heard that some residents complained that they paid the taxes but their kids couldn't use the pool. I returned to the park that day and walked along the dike. I could still imagine her voice and her warm hand in mine. I knew that this, too, would soon be gone. I stood on the dike and watched the muddy river slither through the heart of my town. I felt lonely and estranged, banished in my own land. I wondered where she was, and how it felt to be Ana.

Beth Spencer – Poetry

## On Writing Again

The unused spigot turning tight
No water but
a strangled gasp, deep
clearing of the line
the hiss and croak
then bursting spray
With no control
the rusty water comes.

Nicole Borg – Poetry

## All Our Stories Begin the Same

Right?
Junior high, on my way to Science B,
anonymous ass-grab. I threw an elbow
but didn't look back. The boys' gym teacher
who wrapped the towel around
my bare shoulders, as I exited the pool
half-naked and dripping.
On the streets of small town America
"Hey, Baby, you want some of this?"
as I walked alone or with a friend
or pushing a toddler in a stroller. The
twenty-something guys at Super Valu
who approached thirteen-year-old me.
They were visiting from New York state,
staying at a hotel, did I want
to come over and party?
Super K-Mart at night—bored.
I thought to practice my Spanish
with an older Hispanic man
shopping for a razor. *Afeitarse*
I said but couldn't conjugate the verb
to shave and we both laughed.
When he grabbed me and pulled
me to him, I was too shocked
to push away. A hard kiss on the mouth.
I fled like a common criminal.
Was angry but only at myself.
Last week of high school,
when my Econ teacher put his hand
on my bare stomach (short shirts all the rage)
my best friend and I agreed it was
*so inappropriate. Not okay.*
She gave me a ride home and
we didn't say anymore.
We never spoke of it again.

Chet Corey – Poetry

# The Promise

That is not the night watch swinging his lantern past our bedroom window. That would be the full moon through scattered clouds. The moon is the bright white of lambkin wool. It wraps itself around tree limbs and trunks, like sweaters made for the entire neighbor family next door of nieces and nephews by their old aunt. None of them fitting, all oversized or short in the sleeve, yet dutifully modeled for their aunt, uncomfortable parents and grandparents, one of whom will have too much Mogen David with dinner. The trees draw closer, like her needlepoint placemats to the aunt's circumspect eye. They're soiled with gravy stains, scorched from ironing, yet brought out every Christmas, like the promise of an extended family at peace. And so the nearsighted old aunt holds her tongue, like the Sugar maples the last of their curled leaves. The youngest grandchild is asked to say dinner prayer. The oak trees step back out of reverence, and the lantern moon swings jauntily off.

Harrison Hurd – Poetry – Honorable Mention Humor

# Looking Over my Shoulder

"What's that story about?" my gal queried,
as her short-clipped fingernail
pointed towards the computer screen.
"Which one?" I asked. "The one about the pig?"
"No," she countered.
"Not that one. The next one down. The one titled
'A Decent Affair'."

How could I answer?
I hadn't much cover.
It was me who'd asked her over to help organize
my convoluted computer files.
I said, "It's fiction."
She said,
"You don't write fiction."
She was right.

Now I only write poems
remorseful poems
but at least I can find them in the files.

Jennifer Hernandez – Fiction

# #SickDay

"Don't be such a martyr," Sheila said. We were finally emerging from the bowels of the Convention Center after eight hours of professional development. Mind-numbing. Soul-crushing.

I had just received a text from my sister, who had miraculously gotten tickets to a matinee performance of *Hamilton* the next afternoon. Tickets had been sold out for weeks and were priced beyond my means as a first-year public school teacher anyway. But Lizzie, golden Lizzie, had somehow scored these tickets from a corporate vendor and was willing to share her ineffable good fortune with me.

The only problem was that I was locked into this three-day training. I'd seen the registration costs, and my principal was part of the site team attending the training. My principal, who was in charge of the observations that would determine my fate as non-tenured staff. I was drowning in student loan debt and had just signed a five-year lease on a new car.

"I can't risk it," I said to Sheila. "I need this job."

At the same time, my chest was constricting, my stomach not right. I had a dull ache in my head from too much information dished out under fluorescent lighting and without adequate stretch breaks. (Why, oh why, do educational trainers never practice what they preach?) I'd already endured two days. I didn't anticipate the third would be any different.

As we pushed open the heavy doors of the Convention Center, we were enveloped by a wall of oppressive heat and humidity. Suddenly, the heavens opened, fluffy white clouds parting to reveal the scorching August sun. It seemed like a sign.

    I gazed transfixed, still moving forward, until I felt my next footstep meet thin air. I'd missed the curb and found myself in a pile on the pavement, shooting pains in my left ankle. Sheila stopped short, crouched down next to me.

    "Oh, my gosh! Are you okay?"

    A small smile spread across my face.

    "I am now," I said. "I am now."

---

Dawn Loeffler – Poetry

## Chewing Myself Apart

My nails are gone again
I lost them somewhere between
"Hello" and "Fuck off"
the distance between
gets shorter each time

Sharon Harris – Poetry

# Things I Fear

I dread winter, snow, icy roads
I hate the fear in my heart

I fear falling on ice
broken bones hiding
beneath a dust of snow
becoming dependent on others
having no say in my future


I hate cruel women, their snarky words
I hate weak men who fall for their charms

I fear falling for someone
broken hearts hiding
behind a handsome face
becoming another casualty
having no say in my future

Vincent O'Connor – Poetry

# First Kiss

I gave her a kiss on
Valentine's Day
that honey-lipped lass
of my just
stirring dreams.

Wordless,
heart weighted,
barely not shaking.
Brazen,
emboldened,
yet painfully shy.

But unlike most girls
who would save such a trinket
a foil-covered taste
to remember me by,

she ate it.

Marlene Mattila Stoehr – Creative Nonfiction
Honorable Mention

# The Behavior Plan

She wore a convenience-cut hairstyle and no makeup with her non-trendy wardrobe: heavy, laced-up shoes, shirt buttoned close to her sausage-form body, Docker-style pants.

While I knew her better than anyone else, I scarcely knew her at all: our school's new Behavior Manager. From the beginning I liked her approach to dealing with a student on a behavior plan. Instead of putting an offender on humiliating display in her office, she met the child on the playground, began to forge trust, build some reason for changed behavior.

My teaching materials were stored close by her office. We began chatting as I loaded my cart to switch ungainly supplies back and forth from the far corners of the school.

Through bits and pieces I learned of her delight in her three children—a son attending a private high school, a daughter in college, the oldest son in the working world. I asked once if she had a husband. Her reply: "Yes, but he's not much of a husband." We never revisited that topic.

She told me about a pen pal she had never met, a woman her age from New Zealand. In a strange chance of fate, her daughter went to New Zealand under a Rotary exchange scholarship. In a fairy tale twist, the daughter visited her mother's pen pal, fell in love with and became engaged to the pen pal's son.

With Not-Much-of-a-Husband providing not much toward private school and college tuition, my friend added a part-time job as a weekend security worker to earn travel costs to the New Zealand wedding, and time to stay and become reacquainted with this long-ago pen pal who had become part of her family.

As happy as was that prospect, my friend's life became increasingly difficult. Her mother suffered multiple problems of aging and no longer could live independently. For a time, Not-Much volunteered, or was dispatched, I know not which, to his mother-in-law's home during the day. My friend stayed there at night. Then the mother, frustrated by her weakening condition but not wishing to move to a care facility, came to her daughter's home to stay. The husband moved to the other house.

The mother's condition further deteriorated. I learned one morning that my friend and her mother made a pact—a behavior plan. The mother would stop all food and medicine; the daughter would not intervene. It was a blunt pronouncement, and I sensed that no one else would know what played out during those final days of the school year. No request for silence was made and no promise given, but silence I kept.

I do not know what guided the family's farewell; there was no public notice of the death, no public funeral. I attended a celebration of life when a few neighbors, another teacher and I were invited to the mother's house for conversation and dessert. The empty home, a vacant shell, waited for my friend's son, who would inherit it.

Susan Niemela Vollmer – Creative Nonfiction

# Small Town Minnesota Night

At fourteen, I wanted to be like the teenaged girl on the cover of my sister's red vinyl jewelry box. This girl, in her fashionable cropped pants, lounged on brightly colored pillows, twirling the phone cord around her finger, while musical notes rose from her radio and danced around her head.

Our family didn't have a telephone, and the white-cased pillow from my bed was neither stylish nor comfortable on the hardwood floor.

As I perched there at night, in my decidedly unfashionable jeans and shirt, part of my wish came true. When the atmosphere was right, my transistor radio would fill my room with music—bringing in radio stations far beyond our small town—WDGY in the cities, or sometimes WLS in Chicago.

The Doors would carry me away on their crystal ship, and the Beatles would haunt me with Eleanor Rigby's tale. Wistful tunes would alternate with hard driving rock, opening unexpected doors, creating longings and confusion, and transporting me far beyond the simple world of that girl on the jewelry box.

Dennis Herschbach – Poetry

## After a Summer of Going Barefoot

Ed's playhouse-sized shoe shop held
a torrent of aromas: glue, and oils,
and tanned leather—material to patch
my boots for the new school year.

His personality as black as his hair,
black grease under his fingernails,
the black look in his eyes
verified to me the rumor
his trade was learned in prison.

With a dull thud as sullen as his face,
his machine punched a needle
through rawhide-tough leather.

He grunted answers to Dad's questions.
"Ed, can you stitch this sole?" *Uugh*
"And this toe needs a patch." *Uugh*
"I'll pick them up on Tuesday." *Uugh*

Tuesday rolled around.
"Got those boots done?" *Uugh*
Ed would slap them on the counter,
shove the ticket at Dad,
who'd fish in his pocket for fifty cents.
"How much for a pair of leather laces?"
Ed pointed at a hand-lettered sign;
Dad forked over another fifteen cents.

In the evening I threaded tanned cords
through my leather boots' eyelets,
tried to balance the smells of Ed's shop
with his bitterness.

## Sue Bruns – Poetry
# Autopsy

You examine me, cut me open
and look inside.
You scrutinize, study, dictate your notes
into a small recording device.

It's all very clinical, sterile.
You are meticulous, noticing the lesion on the inside of my
        right knee
and its similarity to one on the inside of my left knee.
You smile a little at the symmetry of these random marks.

You trace the scar on my shoulder with your finger,
the shorter one on my forehead,
and the longer scar on my abdomen.
Compared to many, I have few scars.

You note every detail, inside and out,
every uniqueness and imperfection.

You can study my cold, lifeless body forever,
but the answer to your question isn't there.

Dawn Loeffler – Poetry

# Yesterday's Sister

he knew four-wheelers
boxing gloves
wrestling

but to the kitchen
he turned
oatmeal chocolate chip cookies
unguarded comfort
familiar

playing house was his game
lace aprons and pearls
to hold the baby
to be in charge

love and kindness dripping
from three-inch heels
painted nails
silk and satin
rubbed between index and thumb
wandering aimlessly into this world

Ryan M. Neely – Creative Nonfiction

# The Cheese

Our preschool was a single room in the basement of a Lutheran church on the other side of town. Town wasn't large. It took two songs from the oldies station, or a single story from Paul Harvey, to make the drive. The preschool room was carpeted and smelled of mildew and old books and stale urine. Our teacher was Miss Campbell. She was as old as my grandmother. She had a smile that never left her face with teeth stained yellow from coffee and metal shining through from some obscure dental work and she smelled like fish and powdered make-up.

On the first day of school, Miss Campbell introduced us to a game: The Farmer in the Dell. She would select one child at random to play the farmer while the rest of us pressed into a group in the center of that dank basement. Then we'd all sing and, during the song, the kid playing the farmer would select someone from the class to play the wife and, as the song went on, each newly selected character got to choose another member from the class. The wife chose a child, the child chose a nurse, the nurse chose a cow (for whatever sense that made). Each newly-chosen member of the farmer's family rushed out to join hands with the others until the entire class formed a circle around one lonely child when they were allowed to shout out the final verse, *the cheese stands alone.*

For three months we played that game, and for three months I stood in the center of a swaying circle of smiling faces. The stinky, unwanted cheese.

When I was ten and we had to put down the family dog, my aunt stood next to me and cried with me, but she didn't experience my grief. When I was twenty and the girl I was certain I would marry left me to prostitute herself for meth, my best friend raged with me, but she didn't experience my anger. When I was thirty and diagnosed with cancer and dying from chemotherapy, my wife held my hand every day in the hospital, but she didn't experience my sickness. All of it was mine alone. Each time I was the cheese standing resolute against the onslaught of cheerful life swaying along on its never-ending course whispering to myself, *We all grieve alone, we all hate alone, we all die alone.*

Despite our human need for interpersonal connection, we experience everything as individuals. By ourselves. And we often analyze our lives in search of those larger-than-life events that shaped who we are—an automobile accident, being accepted to an ivy league college, or a beating from your father when you were eleven, perhaps—but we tend to overlook those smaller moments, the quiet times when a single whisper might have changed our entire personality. Decades of tragedy have proven to me that being the cheese was the defining whisper of my life.

Norma Thorstad Knapp – Fiction

# Paddling Her Canoe

Bree hadn't realized how scared she'd been until the sun rose, casting a melon color on everything. Sitting on cold, crumbling cement steps in a strange city, she felt for the motel keys in her jeans' pocket. The rising fog had provided a cocoon, insulating her from further fear.

Sad eyes together with the tremor in her chin and the slope of her fourteen-year-old shoulders suggested she'd been long-acquainted with loss and sorrow. Smelling the scent of rain, she shivered, wrapped her arms around herself, and waited. Her straw-colored hair hung straight, covering her cheeks. Exhausted, she let her mind drift home, a thousand miles away.

Instead of days, it seemed like months ago, that she'd spent the day at her friend Gen's house where they had played Truth and Beauty Shop. Curling Gen's mother's hair, Bree asked Nora, "If George Clooney *seriously* asked you to spend the night with him, would you?" Bree never remembered Nora's answer, only her laughter.

With Gen and Nora, teasing flowed easily. Bree soaked up their joy.

Biting her fingertips and stifling a yawn, Bree stared at the clock on the Spokane National Bank across the street. 6:18 a.m. Questions raced through her mind. *Why can't I have a normal mom? What will they do with her?*

She dozed, then jumped when footsteps tapped. A gentle voice warmed her; sparkling gray eyes encouraged.

"Girl, you must be cold. Come in. I'm Sarah, a social worker. And you?"

"Bree. Breana." Her voice was thick.

"Breana," Sarah repeated softly.

Tears danced in the corners of Bree's eyes as she followed the sandy-haired woman. She scolded herself. *Do not cry.*

Sarah led her into a small, pleasant room filled with plump, sage-colored sofas and gray walls decorated with yellow daisies.

"Get comfortable. Back in a bit."

As Bree sank into one sofa, Sarah peeked around the doorway.

"I have bagels, doughnuts, milk."

Bree jumped, a croak in her voice. "Doughnuts . . . milk."

"Sit!" Sarah ordered, her hands bobbing. She walked down the hallway, her heels echoing.

Roaming the room, Bree wrung her hands. On one wall, a photo of a family flying kites held an inscription: "Some days are made for playing." Somewhere in the distance, Pat Benatar sang about everything falling in line.

*Will Sarah believe me? Listen to me? Why did I go with Mom in the first place?*

Bree slowly sucked in deep breaths like Nora taught her, then blew them out. When she began to chant, *Breathe, breathe,* a rhythm started within her.

Events of the past seventy-two hours reeled through her mind. She tried putting the pieces together.

Three hours later, it was over. Bree's face was ashen, tear-stained. Sipping her milk, she'd given herself up to memory. Sarah sat back in her chair, calm.

Bree told how they'd left Minnesota three days ago when her mom was well . . . how her mom had slowly broken down . . . how she'd begun not looking like herself, not acting like herself . . . like a madman: accusatory, mean . . . how she'd tried to hurt herself . . . how she'd threatened Bree . . . how she'd ranted and raved . . . how over the Rockies she'd tried to drive off the road . . . tried to kill them both . . . no, she didn't know why . . . how Bree had to drive, find a town, a motel . . . how she'd kept her mom in that motel room . . . how she'd decided what to do . . . no, her dad had never wanted her . . .

Later Sarah, a policeman, and Bree arrived at the motel where Bree's mother slept. They admitted her to a psychiatric hospital. Hugging Breana, Sarah said, "Honey, we each are paddling our canoes best we know how."

At the depot, Sarah waited with Bree for the bus to take her back to Minnesota. To Nora's house. Nora's name had been ready on Bree's lips. It'd taken Sarah the entire day, planning arrangements. Bree hoped she'd make a good impression.

The bus arrived; smells of diesel settled everywhere. When they reached simultaneously to say goodbye, Bree tasted salty tears freely flowing down her cheeks.

As the bus jerked into motion, Bree walked to a back seat, watching the tired sun slump in the west, like it was turning toward more people needing light.

Carla Hagen – Poetry

# The Bike Locker

She watches me unload my bike,
December morning, still balmy
but cold coming.

Does not beg for change
or a buck for the bus.
Stares at the locker,

pie-shaped plastic slice,
mine to rent through
winter—which I

defy with studded tires,
goggles, Merino wool
face mask—

wants to see inside, how
wide it is, how tall,
vented in front.

Has questions: does the wall
fold down? Is it big
enough?

*For my bike*, I say.

Stephen Sinicrope – Poetry
## I Play Violin

Because what separates mankind from the rest
is that we use tools, like a bow
on strings that can drown out sorrow
without shooting anything.
Because sound adds color to sensing
bodies, helping us listen more, speak less.
Because my soul sails the strings, magically
mirrors thoughts as I play, omnisciently aware.
Because communication is easier in waves
and an orchestra needs leaders in song.
Because trees gave their flesh for these natural vibrations
ringing to the core, holding you in a hypnotic embrace.
Because it bleeds with your tears.

Charmaine Pappas Donovan – Poetry

# Walk Among Fallen Leaves
*for Jimmy Nichols*

You never wore
sentiment on your sleeve,
left like a fugitive under night
telling no one your plans—
a late date with the carbon monoxide
trapped in your closed garage.

None of us knew
what you would do
when you received the diagnosis:
throat cancer.
You saw first-hand
the disfiguring effects
of surgery
repeated radiation
disappearance of voice
from your work in Radiology.

I barely make out the bird
blending into fall leaves
—tears on the trail unavoidable—
as this odd sparrow
stills, lets me bend near.
I almost touch his feathers,
so close, as close as memories.

J. Mackenzie – Creative Nonfiction
## Early Winter Sky

My dad couldn't convince me to pull my pants on over my shorts, though he did make me put my coat on before leaving the gym.

"How was practice?" he asked as we walked to the car.

"Fine," I replied. I'd just discovered the power of this monosyllable and its ability to hide so many things.

In truth, practice had been . . . confusing. I was the only girl on a co-ed team, which had never been a problem, least of all for me. I'd never understood the point in separating us into different leagues.

Up to today, the only reason my teammates had for treating me differently was because I was significantly worse than everyone else. A certain air would go out of the room when I dribbled up for a shot. There was a resignation. *Maybe we'd get points on the next play.* But I was running and laughing and trying. I was still *playing* basketball, and I didn't care if I wasn't good at it.

But today was different. Today, we learned how to screen, or block, a player without getting a foul. The basic idea is to get your arms out of the way. My coach extended his arms long, locked his elbows straight in front of him and folded his hands. I'd seen my uncles stand similarly at my great-grandma's funeral, when putting your hands in your pockets was too informal. We all tried it, but then he looked at me and shook his head.

He said, "No, you do this." He thought for a moment, and then awkwardly crossed his arms across his chest, like he'd never given himself a hug before. We'd done it all the time, in kindergarten. But it seemed silly to do now. I wasn't sure what this was supposed to do. If it was to provide my body with any sort of protection, I might as well have done what the boys were doing. There was nothing on my ten-year-old body to protect.

I still felt the awkwardness of this moment in the back of my dad's car. To that point, I'd been able to shirk off the differences between boys and girls, choosing to do whatever I'd wanted. But this was a difference that I couldn't ignore.

I looked out the window, up to the December sky. Shining brightly above me were three stars, perfectly in a row. I wondered how that happened, and if anyone else had ever noticed this small phenomenon before.

*Everything will be okay*, went through my head. I didn't recognize the voice. But I understood then that this was the way of things. They'd seen this all before, these three sister stars, and I could feel their timelessness held up against my brief breath of an existence. The top star winked at me, and assured me that they'd guide me through this, and the many changes that were to come beneath this winter's sky.

Niomi Rohn Phillips – Poetry

# Remembering Paradise
*in Heartland Manor*

from the window of her room
she gazes at the prairie meeting the sky
she sees blue . . . blue-green ocean touching clouds

the scene unfolds behind the scrim

she treks down the cliff to Secret Beach
the rhythmic crash of waves growing louder
with her descent to the shore

she feels the whisper of wing brushing her forehead
an albatross swooping
then soaring to its cliff-side nest

she discovers a perfect shell in the sand
a flash of joy breaks into her emptiness
a fleeting smile

she runs her hands through the puka shells
cradles each cone and cowrie . . . fondles the feather
in the coconut-leaf basket in her lap

## Peter Stein – Poetry
## Love Letters

I am locked inside a vault of words
   that have no meaning
      other than what an old white man
         has ascribed to them

They are how I relate to
   the outside world

      you are the outside world


I write messages on paper airplanes
   and throw them out the window

Did you get my message?

I have yet to hear back
   so I float note after note
      out the hole in the wall

using every possible permutation of words
   and hope this time

      you understand

Frances Ann Crowley – Creative Nonfiction

# Shoe Shine

It was almost time for my seventh-grade year to begin. I had been attending Walker #21, a country school about five miles from the ranch. Now I would be going to town school. I had two burning questions: What would I wear? What about my hair?

My best friends were sisters from a neighboring ranch and when we got together that August, we were all about new shoes. My friends are from strong German stock, tall and big-boned. There are no sons in their family, so the girls were expected to take up the slack. They milked cows (by hand) and spent long days on tractors or horses. They were good riders.

My heritage is Irish and I am short, fine-boned, and freckled. I have a brother. I was a good reader and I played the piano at Farm Bureau meetings and Sunday school. I spent my chore time in the garden or the kitchen. But, I wanted to be like my friends and envied everything they had.

The sisters were excited about the new Glovets they would be getting. I had never seen Glovets, but the name was so elegant. I had to have them, too. When I asked my mother if I could get a pair for school, she gave me a strange look. She must have been wondering why the girly-girl, who asked for every impractical item in the Sears catalog, wanted them. She suggested saddle shoes. I needed Glovets.

On back-to-school shopping day, we made a trip to Isaac's Mercantile. The first thing I saw in the shoe department was a display of saddle shoes. I was almost persuaded. Then I saw the G-word on a box and remembered my dearest wish. My mom asked Martha, the mercantile owner, if she had a size five. Martha said she did, then climbed a ladder and brought down the magic box. When she popped the lid, my inner child gasped. If OMG had existed, it would have occupied the thought bubble above my head.

Not about to admit ignorance, I pretended to still want the ugliest shoes ever made. Of course, I *had* seen Glovets before. They were plain, old oxfords. I know my mother saw me cringe. My guess is that she decided it was a good time for one of those pesky life lessons.

I wore my Glovets every school day that year and, in them, took one giant step toward getting over myself. I found that I still loved reading and writing. My English teacher chose my essay for the prime spot on the bulletin board for parent-teacher conferences. I still played the piano and I made some new friends. I also learned what my mother meant when she said, "Be careful what you wish for . . ."

Neil Dyer – Poetry

# One morning walking to the bus

The moon is
full, fogged
as a cataract;
the streetlight,
a drupe hanging
from a fluted post
behind me, shedding
light, cantilevered
and casting a
second shadow, my
doppelganger, the
three of
us, scissored dolls,
walking hand in
hand to the bus

Jean Scoon – Poetry – Honorable Mention Humor

# That Suit

She took in sewing those days, she said.
Single mom, husband nowhere in sight,
she needed the money.

"I'll never forget, my neighbor once gave me a piece of silk,"
she told me.
"This silk! I'd never felt anything as smooth and lovely.
I could just see it as part of a man's suit. You know, the vest.
How it's lined."

She decided to make a suit, all three pieces.
For her oldest; he was starting to date.

"I'd never made one before, but I imagined him
looking so handsome in that suit.
And there was no other way he'd get one back then."

She had to save for months and
wait for three sales to buy the rest of the fabric.

"I already knew how to sew, of course. But that suit!
It was more complicated than I expected."

It took weeks in the library,
learning from magazines, sewing books
while she made it.

Lapels, top stitching, they were all new to her.
Even so, she was determined to get it right.

"I did a good job.
But when he put it on, I could only laugh.
He'd already outgrown it."

Beth L. Voigt – Creative Nonfiction
# The Christmas Marathon

It felt like a marathon. Between December 19 and December 25, my senior year in high school, I ran.

When I walked in the door on the 19th, the start gun fired. "Your mother broke her leg," Dad said. "I'll need more help from you for a while."

"Is she okay? Where is she?"

"She is resting in bed. She's on pain killers." He put on his suit coat. "I'm going back to the office."

"Wait, how . . ."

"She slipped on the ice in the driveway." He adjusted his shirt collar. "I'll be ready to eat at 6 p.m."

The first mile and I had no idea what lay ahead of me.

I tiptoed down the hall and peeked into my parents' room.

"Mom, how are you feeling?" Her left leg, encased in a cast, was propped up on two pillows.

"Just a small setback." She handed me a crumpled piece of paper. "I wrote down what each of you can help me with. Gail can drive and cook, Brian grocery shop, Joni dishes, Eric babysit and bedtime stories, Paul vacuum and bathrooms, Myra laundry and you Christmas shopping," which she always reserved for the week before Christmas. She handed me another piece of paper.

When did she write them? While she was on her way to the hospital? Waiting for X-rays? While the cast was drying?

I counted 42 names on the list. Size 4T and books for Marci. Size 5 and a stuffed horse for Nori (each year she asked for a real horse but received a facsimile instead). Size 8 and a nurse's kit for Myra. My brothers' names just had sizes listed. My aunts' names had mostly household items listed. My uncles' names were all followed by the word "sweater." My dad's name was followed by a question mark.

"Start your shopping at Sears downtown," she said as she closed her eyes. "They usually have good deals, especially on sweaters."

The race was heating up. For the next few days, mile after mile, Dad doled out the cash early in the morning, and I shopped and reported my purchases to Mom late at night.

Mom cheered me on. "I know it's a lot of work, honey, but you can do it," she said.

By December 24, I had purchased all of the gifts, heaped in piles on my parents' bedroom floor. Then I began to wrap, unfurling rolls upon rolls of colorful paper as Mom, from her bed, affixed name tags to each gift.

On Christmas Day, when my siblings rushed to show off their new toys and modeled their new outfits, and my family feasted on our only potluck Christmas dinner on paper plates, I sat quietly beside Mom on the sofa—both of us with our feet propped up on the coffee table. She said, "This has been the most relaxing Christmas ever!" I floppily raised my hands above my head, as if crossing the finish line in victory.

Elizabeth Weir – Poetry

# Fabric

I wouldn't have called it burlap—
not exactly. No. It was more
common cotton, thin thread,
plain and a bit worn. But comfortable.

By chance, silk happened along.
Charming, yes, a cocoon of love
and new well-being but, oh,
the effort to keep it pressed.

If you are cotton, true to your core,
can you ever do more than
slip on filmy silk, assume
your place with taut grace?

And always that slight tug, lonely
for the close-woven hug
of coarser cloth, the complete ease
of family homespun.

Richard Fenton Sederstrom – Poetry

# Life Outside Prague

Mozart's Prague Symphony fails as it always fails
in my distracted earshot. Today, the symphony
fails to compete with my neighbor's chainsaw.

The distractions today discompose a polychordant
                    cacophony.
Chuck finishes cutting up the corpse of a drought-starved
                    birch tree.
I am in time to witness the final cut.

Then Chuck's combustion-performance intermits.
I look up to see the last fat cylinder of white birch log
roll away from him and lumber

toward the dirt road we share, and I hear in a chainsaw-
                    breve
that I have missed a few bars of the great symphony.
Thus:

Mozart has failed to compete
with this afternoon's noisy attentions to duty. That is,
Mozart, rising, has failed again to enter the competition
                    with us.

The Prague had risen above us all from the very start,
and it has remained where it started,
never so lofty that it soars above my attention.

The birch log rolls and rolls
and it is all part of the white memory that will occupy me
in the un-codified silence of the real peace of my day.

Christina Joyce – Creative Nonfiction

# Salvation

"If you give me your ice cream, you'll go to heaven."

My older brother Mike's words hung in the warm August air, heavy with the promise of eternal salvation. We sat side-by-side at the redwood picnic table, clutching our cones and enjoying the last free moments before bedtime. We were wrapped in darkness except for a rectangle of light shining through the dining room windows. I could hear my parents inside rounding up my three younger brothers for pre-bedtime baths.

The ice cream numbed my tongue as I cut a soft trail into the frozen mounds of vanilla, slowly winding my way to the summit. Descending, I erased the newly formed ridges before beginning another ascent on a slightly smaller peak. Mike preferred chomping, a style of eating he had perfected during his nine years of life. His cone disappeared in less time than it took for Mom to make it.

"If you give me your ice cream, you'll go to heaven," Mike repeated, obviously concerned about the fate of my soul. Ever since Uncle Louie died suddenly a few weeks before, death was our favorite topic of conversation. Or, more accurately, what happens *after* death.

How could I be sure I would go to heaven when I died? I was fresh from first grade and listening to Sister Michael Ann, shrouded in black veils, solemnly recite a catalog of sins that children were prey to. These included the unholy trinity of misdeeds: disobeying your parents, wasting food and coveting your friends' stuff. If I had only a few sins blotting my soul when I died, I could look forward to purgatory, a kind of detention center for the dead. If, however, I had a stockpile of marks against me, I would go directly to hell and spend an eternity contemplating my wrongdoings. (Having endured twenty minutes of forced silence—punishment for talking during Mass—I had a good idea of how long eternity was.) Clearly, my soul was in peril.

And now, here was Mike with insider information on the Afterlife. That he knew what he was talking about, I had no doubt: he had already made his First Communion and Confirmation and gained all the power those sacraments bestowed.

I leaned back, looking at the stars, and wondered where Uncle Louie was. In life, he was a shadowy figure, another grown-up who occasionally passed through our small world. In death, he opened a new universe to us, one that was mysterious and scary and thrilling.

The whine of a mosquito in my ear turned my thoughts earthward. I heard my parents' voices through the dining room windows and my younger brothers trying to negotiate a few more minutes of play before going to bed.

Before Mike asked a third time, I handed him my ice cream cone. We all had deals to make before we slept.

Lina Belar – Poetry

# Crossroads

Driving the back roads
of west central Minnesota
it's impossible not to notice
how many signs point to Wolf Lake.

The town itself is small,
with a newly remodeled gas station,
an active VFW club,
several abandoned buildings.

The Kinnunen general store
is closed and shuttered,
its third and last letters
missing for decades.

At the crossroads, signs
point to other distant towns.
All roads lead to Wolf Lake;
All roads leave here, too.

Michael Kiesow Moore – Poetry

# Do not reject the world

Why is it so easy
to say, no not
this? I want it
different. Not
what I asked for.
Not my world.

Can I cup my hands
to the runnels of
regret, let the
sharp shards
of rejection
sit in my palm?

I want to say, this
is how it is, tell
my reflection, you
are fine, there is
nothing wrong. We
are all good here.

Ben Westlie – Poetry

# My Dazzler

I remember the joyful chaos of carnivals—the congregation of chance games and the too-loud laughter of surrounding strangers. Above me in the distant sky, human arms and massive wheels spinning elevated in flight—a brew of togetherness among the clouds. I remember my need for a snow cone and how I thought I could taste colors and not just flavors. How even the air I breathed in seemed deep-fried and my mouth's merriment and then my skin like butter—my pores full of sun. I remember her in that circular-linked home rounding in one place over and over in a sparkling carousel. My metal horse I named Dazzler. Her petal pink mane, her matching magenta saddle, her body shimmering like moonlight caught in snow. Her eyes stunned in the surprise of rubies and her hoofs glittering gold as if she would never tarnish. I remember the fear I had of her fakeness. That if she knew how as a little boy I wanted to be pretty and somehow glow even in a crowd like she could, I would be nothing close to a man, someday. I kept silent as she and I went in countless turns, my dizziness alluring. I soared somewhere closer to the stars as the day transformed into night and the carnival became a constellation surrounding me with all of its light.

Nicole Borg – Poetry
## Summer Ending, Summer Over

I examine my bare legs,
shaved summer-smooth,
the purple veins branching behind knees.
Waist, too thick by my standards.
A frantic spring—new job—
too little sleep, too many venti sugars
extra shot of caffeine, please, barista.
Forty-one and still my eye on the mirror
scrutinizes gray strands and laugh lines,
spots on my hands that aren't freckles.
The small spill of my belly over jeans—
I pretend it's nothing really.

You'd think I'd be done—
strong woman—
mother, teacher, writer.
Yet I'm married to the physical
the curving silhouette, the satin-skinned
selfie, profile picture of me in makeup,
hair ironed smooth.
This power youth brings
I cling to it. In grad school,
Professor Varhely said
*you can only look twenty ten years;*
I'm past that by miles.
And I think—how beautiful
it would be to let it all go.
How terrifying.

Tenlee Lund – Fiction

# Sisters?

I knew it! We aren't really sisters! I stared at the papers in my shaking hands—DNA results that could not have come from sisters.

All the years of having to look out for Lisa. She was so gentle and artistic, so pretty and fragile, not a workhorse like me, not a racehorse like Cindy. Lisa was Mom's favorite, always so different from Cindy and me. Now I was beginning to understand why.

Our family history is a tangle of hearsay and myth and, at this point, there is no one left to untangle it. Our parents died in a car accident when we were children and we were raised by an unhappy grandmother and a bitter aunt. The acrimonious situation made the thought of delving into our ancestry unappealing. No one talked about it and no one asked.

No one cared, either, until we got older. Now all three of us were middle-aged and there is no one left to ask. Our grandparents and older relatives are all gone but I knew—I KNEW!—that something was amiss, and now technology offered a glimmer of hope. Television ads touted ways to trace ancestry. Maybe this would clarify everything once and for all.

"Oh, come on, let's try it! What have we got to lose?" I cajoled as Lisa and I were having coffee. I had no idea what would come of it. Now I was holding copies of two distinctly different DNA reports, one hers, one mine.

Talk about knocking the lid off of Pandora's box. Maybe I should have left well enough alone. We both knew our parents "had to get married." Back in the 1950s, that's what you did under such circumstances. As their lives progressed their family grew, first Lisa, then me, then Cindy.

Then it fell apart and things went from bad to worse.

At her first opportunity Cindy headed for parts unknown, eventually landing in Alaska. Lisa and I stayed closer to home and each other, as some sisters do—and now I wasn't even sure we were really "sisters." After all, what did the term "sister" really mean?

Instead of clearing things up, this DNA techno-intrusion had turned everything upside-down. Instead of answering questions, it raised many more. Instead of feeling vindicated, I felt tremendously guilty.

Lisa had always been the trail-blazer, the one who learned things first and then taught me. We walked to school together, did the dishes together, took dancing and piano lessons together, consoled each other and Cindy when things were rough at home. Lisa had been there for more than half a century. How could she not be my sister? Did it really matter if we had different fathers (as I surmised)? Wasn't there more to being a "sister" than shared DNA?

And how was I ever going to tell her what I was thinking? I felt like the ultimate traitor. How could I face this—or ignore it? My mental wrestling match continued until Cindy's letter arrived. When I'd told her Lisa and I were doing the DNA test, she apparently had decided to do one, too.

And for the second time in a week, my world turned upside-down. Once again staring at papers in my shaking hands, I slowly started to comprehend Cindy's DNA report matched Lisa's, not mine. I'd been so sure but I'd been wrong—mine was the one that was different.

I guess I'd always felt like an outsider; now I knew why. I'd resented Lisa's talent and beauty, Cindy's confidence and zest for life, never feeling like I quite fit in—because I didn't.

Margaret M. Marty – Poetry

# Obsession

Today I should really
clean the house,
It's been a while—
but first I'll find the cat.

And my desktop
is piled high with mail
and undone filing,
but first I'll feed the cat.

I should go outdoors
to start the spring cleanup,
put the deck furniture out,
after I freshen his litter box.

He loves when I play piano,
so I'll play a few tunes
as he sits by me on the bench,
purring his own melody.

There's laundry to do
and dishes to put away.
but he's begging me to throw
the toy he loves to retrieve.

In between times, he needs
lots of stroking, along with
words of love over and over—
precious, darling, sweetie pie.

His favorite time of all?
Our daily rendezvous—
he curls up against my back
while we take our afternoon
nap.

Jeanne Emrich – Poetry

# Overnight

It was silence that woke me up.
Overnight, ice shut down the pond
and the restless geese left,
their wings ripping the blue-black air.
I never heard them leave.

It was silence that woke me up.
Look, everyone loses something.
Everyone moves on. I only thought
to witness that joined moment
when all moved as one and to the south.
I only envied them.

It was silence that woke me up.
I thought of the young, strong enough
now for the journey on tested wings.
It is something to be born
into such a family and grow into
unimagined, miraculous strength.
I only envied them.
I never heard them leave.

Kim A. Larson – Fiction

# A Do-Over

"I'm so proud of you, Jordyn." Mom wriggled next to me in the front seat of Old Betty. "I knew you could pass your driver's test. You're such a talented young lady."

"Thanks." I buckled Mom's seatbelt, wishing she had been this excited for me ten years ago when it had actually happened.

Though I hadn't seen Mom in years, Abby, my sister, had insisted I take Mom home at precisely eight p.m. I asked if Mom would turn into a pumpkin, and Abby said a pumpkin would be far more pleasant. This tempted me to drive around until I conjured up a feisty Mom instead of the depressed one I knew growing up. But I didn't.

A few minutes later, I pulled into the garage and parked next to Mom's red Mustang convertible. Its purchase two years ago alerted Abby to Mom's failing mental health. I whistled, admiring the car. "Nice wheels."

She shrugged. "It was your father's idea, not mine." Mom seldom remembered their divorce, among other things. Abby had encouraged me to play along with whatever Mom said. I let the time warp slide, but I couldn't commit to living with her in La La Land.

Once inside, Mom made a beeline for the living room. I followed and froze in the doorway. Hordes of little bodies had overtaken the room. Mom busied herself tending to the baby dolls lining the floor and furniture.

I retreated to the dining room and called Abby. "Hey, what's going on? Did you forget to tell me about the additions to our family?"

Abby broke into laughter.

I gritted my teeth. "Where'd she get them? I thought you took away her checkbook after the car fiasco."

"Come on, Jordyn, laugh." Abby still was, and so hard I could hardly understand her. "If you don't, you'll cry."

*No. I won't.* "Seriously, Abbs, where'd she get them?"

"QVC. Aren't they adorable? They look so real."

"Holy crap. They scared me half to death. It was like stepping into *Invasion of the Body Snatchers*." I managed a weak laugh. "How'd she buy them?"

"I missed a credit card somewhere. But I've got it now."

I blew out a long breath. "You could've sent them back."

"I didn't have the heart to. She had them all unpacked, bundled in dishtowels and hand towels, and was hovering over them like a mother hen. I hadn't seen her that happy in years. Granted, I freaked out at first, too. But when I even suggested sending a few back, she cried inconsolably." Abby sighed. "It's only money, right? If it makes Mom happy caring for them, who are we to deprive her?"

"A little warning would have been nice."

"What fun would that have been?" Abby snickered. "Now you know why Mom needed to get home. She has a meltdown if she can't hold her babies before bed. Or at least I assume she goes to bed. I've read she may soon be up at night wandering around."

"Oh, great, something more to scare me: a night stalker."

"See why I need your help? She's more than I can handle alone."

"I'll support whatever you decide about her care, but

I'm not moving home. I've got leads on another job."

After ending the conversation, I tiptoed back to the living room. Mom was talking baby gibberish to a curly-haired brunette doll cradled in her arms. "I love you so much, Jordyn." She pulled the baby to her chest. "You're the joy of my life, and I will never let anything bad happen to you."

If only she'd have been that loving and protective of the *real* me. My heart ached. Why couldn't Dad have stuck around? At least until I'd finished grade school. Maybe Mom wouldn't have been so depressed.

She began singing a sweet lullaby. Where had I heard that before? My eyes stung as I remembered. She'd sung this to me every night before bed—until their divorce.

I drew near to Mom and rested my head on her shoulder. If she could attempt a do-over, shouldn't I at least try?

Susan Perala-Dewey – Poetry
# Solstice Sky

Venus rises early
Dancing on the June horizon
Pacing her orbit for the long light

She flashes a smile as we
Clear, strip, wrangle roots from hard soil
Dig in and spend our endless energy

. . . when new growth emerges alive and wild

She whispers *lean back into love*
Toward new stars twinkling
Expanding our universe once again.

New Arrangements

Joy Saethre – Creative Nonfiction

# The Hope Chest

"I'm moving out at the end of the month," I announced to my parents.

My dad didn't even look up from the television and stated, "You're not eighteen yet."

My mother snickered. She sat in her recliner with a cigarette between her yellow stained fingers. Beside her was her usual glass of Pepsi, chocolate fudge, a paperback crime novel and an ashtray overflowing with butts. "How are you going to cook without pans? What about dishes or towels? You're not taking mine!"

"I'll figure something out," I mumbled.

My father said, "I thought you wanted to go to college. You can't go if you move out."

I hadn't thought about that. I was already registered for the Fall semester, but I needed to move out.

"Where are you going to live? What about utilities? Or a phone? I bet you didn't think about that. Did you?" my mother taunted. "Well, don't ask us for money. We can't help you." My mother picked up her book. My father watched TV. I was dismissed.

I padded down the hall to my room and shut the door. At the foot of my bed was my cedar hope chest. I unlocked it and examined each item: plush bath towels, cotton dishcloths, dinnerware, Teflon-coated pans, knives, utensils, an electric mixer, mixing bowls, spatulas, wooden spoons, measuring cups, bars of soap, toilet paper, and my pink porcelain pig filled with $2000 cash. I even acquired an old couch, a coffee table and a kitchen table and chairs. They were being stored at my best friend's house. I guess deep down I always knew my decision.

On moving day, my best friend's boyfriend backed his pickup into the driveway. As we struggled with the heavy furniture down the hall, my parents sat quietly side by side on the couch like they were in a pew at a funeral staring at the blaring television. Even when we dropped the dresser with a thud or banged the headboard into the wall, they didn't look up or make a peep. When we finished loading everything into the truck, I went back inside to say goodbye.

"Well, I guess I've got everything," I said cheerfully. "I'll try to call you every day and let you know how I'm doing."

Only the sound of the television blasted into the icy room.

"Okay . . . I guess I'm gonna go now."

Silence.

"Well, Ma, now you can finally have your own art room."

My mother bit her lip. My dad said, "We'll keep your room empty for when you come back."

My smile disappeared. I turned on my heel and stomped from the living room. No hugs. No kisses. No encouraging words. I felt cheated. I opened the kitchen door and looked back once more. They hadn't followed me. From the living room came the soft sound of sniffles like soldiers who had lost the battle. I brushed back a tear. "I won't be back."

Georgia A. Greeley – Poetry

# Bird's Wings

The whistler flies so low
she almost skims the river's surface

Is so close to moisture
she almost drinks the air she breathes

Her golden eyes gleam
with the movement of all she touches—

sun
water
air

willing wings beat like the earth's heart—

beat, I am
beat, I can
beat, she's gone

I stand in silence
wanting to hear what no longer sounds

My own heart echoing
the song of a bird's wings

Tim J. Brennan – Poetry

# Another Morning You Doubt Yourself

When the sun rises, she will be here,
remaining even after you say,
*No, this isn't working.*

She laughs and asks with a voice
like a canyon, *Will you write
another poem about us?*

Suddenly, she is emerald water,
her tide coming close to you,
a champion of concealment.

It has never been easy—
your past a whisper of ground glass

and like a child, twisting
gently on a seat with thin chains,
she may be gone before you know it.

Susan McMillan – Poetry

# Steamy

A steamy relationship
starts with fueling of a stove
an hour or so before—
crumpled paper, kindling sticks,
the breath of bellows.
    It lacks
any outside power—no electricity
or shower. Instead
        little room
intrinsic scent of primal smoke, musk
of smooth unfinished cedar,
hint of pine or eucalyptus oil
wafted from a wooden pail.

    In what it lacks
it lacks nothing as we two alone
bare but for bathrobes and summer sandals
pad our way in silence on a snowlit path
to this little shack among the trees.
        We defy
prying neighbors' eyes and eyes
of covert rodents in the dark.

    Shuck your robe,
I'll hang it from the iron hook
outside the hand-hewn door—its little window
facing up into the wooded hill. Find
your favorite spot on the high bench now.
Take the wooden ladle,
        spoon cool water over rocks,
then close your eyes and rest beside me
    skin to sweating skin.

Norita Dittberner-Jax – Poetry

# Monet: The Demarcation of Light

Living so close, he would have walked with his easel and
        paints
to Paris Saint-Lazare and set up, in full view

of the open train shed, that magnificent arrow
pointing out to the world. Eleven times, he painted it,

billowing steam rising to the skylight, vaporous fog,
the gray light of Paris, the atmospherics of light and water.

An interlude between Argenteuil and Giverny, between
        field
and flower, the trains, wheels, gears, the manmade madness

of Paris and he right in the middle of it. Did anyone stop
to question the loose brushstrokes? They veered past him

hurrying to the gate. He ignored them, too, painted them
        thin
strokes of black paint beside the belching engine.

Jeanne Everhart – Fiction – Honorable Mention

# Haunted

"Don't go there, Mom!" my daughter warned. Curiosity made me type "haunted doll" on my computer. Browsing the Web, pictures of grotesque dolls, pleasant dolly faces and stories of diabolic spirit-possessed dolls make the hair stand up on the back of my neck. It says dolls are a favorite object for departed spirits to inhabit.

The urge to open the door of my doll museum, as my daughter calls the room, is irresistibly uncanny. My hand on the doorknob, senses acutely aware, I look around the room filled with baby dolls in buggies and cradles, dolls sipping tea in miniature kitchens, fashion dolls poised for the runway, celebrity and storybook dolls. In carefully arranged dioramas are dolls from around the world, antique porcelains, Madame Alexanders and hundreds more, staring at me. Turning off the lights, I leave the windowless room, shut the door, and laugh at my vivid imagination.

The next morning, every doll is in her place. Was I expecting something different? Just as I breathe a sigh of relief, I notice an old composition doll tipped over. I sit her back up, survey the room and leave, closing the door tightly.

My cat is my shadow as housework occupies my mind until early afternoon. I visit my doll room again. Somehow Alice in Wonderland has toppled from her shelf. I ask, "What are you doing on the floor?" She gives me a blank stare. I straighten the blue dress and white apron, smooth her blonde hair and place her beside the Queen of Hearts.

Feeling a little silly, I remark, "Everyone behave and stay where you belong tonight." My guardian angel cat is waiting for me just outside the door. Stretching her neck, she peers curiously inside the room. Ears flattened, she sniffs, and her tail bristles as she flies past me down the hall. I tell myself not to think about the haunted website anymore and enjoy my dolls.

Tuesday morning as I walk through, the early 1900s composition, Bubbles, stares with bulging eyes in an unnerving way. Did I put Raggedy Ann there? I don't remember Chatty Cathy being behind Grow Hair Crissy. I'm letting my imagination get away from me. Don't be paranoid. There are too many dolls to keep track of them all.

Wednesday morning, I glance at the clock for no particular reason and decide to do a "walk through." My antique porcelain doll Ella is tipped over. Rearranging the mohair wig, I notice a hairline crack by her ear. "What happened?" I ask. Beside her sits a lovely 1800s porcelain Handwerck doll with brown ringlets of human hair. I wonder who once was adorned by those lovely long curls. Because of her smile, I named her Mona Lisa. Her big, brown glass eyes were mesmerizing when I bought her at the auction. I couldn't believe no one wanted this beautiful antique doll. I had been prepared to bid double what I paid for her. As I gaze at her eyes now, imagination overcomes me. "Her eyes and expression were frozen since the day she was created, you silly old woman," I whisper to myself. An eerie feeling comes over me. I stand waiting, slowly turning my head to catch movement from the corner of my eye. All is quiet. The mouth of the ventriloquist doll suddenly gapes open as I turn in his direction. Hundreds of eyes, staring straight ahead, seem to be waiting for me to leave so they can blink. Claustrophobia engulfs me. I hasten out the door.

Why had family members left the antique Handwerck doll behind? Was she haunted? I dressed her in a filmy white antique child's dress, also purchased at the auction. *What is the history of that little girl's dress?* I wonder. Mona is a beautiful apparition of a seventeenth-century child. I should never have looked at that paranoia-spawning website. My dolls no longer give me pleasure.

Brown-eyed Mona Lisa must go. With some regret, I said goodbye, leaving her with the auctioneer. Everything stayed in place in the doll room. No more tip-overs and once again I enjoy showing people the collection. The room feels welcoming. These inanimate objects are only toys—memories of another period of time.

This morning I complete my walk-through smiling, reach to turn the lights out and leave. Chatty Cathy's tiny voice calls, "Mama." I close the door quickly behind me, shaking my head to bring back reality.

Julie Chattopadhyay – Poetry

# In Honor of Liz Adams, 1927-2017

The pond absorbed the darkened spring sky,
more like oil than water.

Bold and far from shore shone a male mallard's iridescent
             head,
audacious and dazzling in the dull landscape.

Although I knew they must be there,
the females' muddy bodies were invisible in the still-brown
             weeds,
encumbered by waddling gaits and hidden nests.

Until one left the others
and I saw her:
silver trail slicing through the water,
a bright, unexpected vector.

Edis Flowerday – Fiction

# Midnight Run

Ever since Phil retired, he'd been plagued by insomnia. In the wee hours, he'd pad down the hall to his office, turn on the computer, and pick a game. Barbara, his wife, always woke in sympathy, but she never got up. One night in mid-January, though—when the temperature was way below zero and their old house made popping noises as it shrank away from the cold—Phil rushed into the bedroom and shook her.

"It's Wes Larkin!" he said. "I saw him jog up the alley, wearing only shorts and shoes! Is the man crazy? He'll freeze to death!"

Wes Larkin had moved up from Florida the previous summer, and this was his first northern winter. He read the news for a local radio station in a beautiful, tenor voice. The neighborhood women, however, felt that radio was wrong for him, a complete waste of his handsome face and buff body. And they likened him to an endearing little kid. At the summer block party, Wes joined the children in the sauna-like interior of the bouncy castle, and came out glistening with sweat. When the fire engine put in its usual appearance, he climbed into the cab, gripped the steering wheel, and made engine noises. Recently, he'd been seen standing in the snow at the bus stop, wearing leather-soled loafers and a London Fog raincoat. Clearly, he needed taking in hand.

That January night Barbara got up and followed Phil back to his office. They peered out the window into the darkness. If they saw Wes staggering home in the throes of hypothermia, how, Barbara wondered, would he react to the commonly accepted remedy: being stuffed naked into a sleeping bag along with another naked person. Perhaps even Barbara, herself.

"It could have been a teenager out on a bet," she said. "You know kids. 'Double-dare me to run down to the lake and back, stark naked.' Are you sure it was Wes?"

"I'm sure, and he *was* practically naked. I'm getting the car to go look for him."

"I'm coming, too," Barbara said.

They pulled on thermal underwear, wool socks, and flannel-lined jeans. They stepped into Sorel boots and bundled into down jackets. On their way out the door, Barbara scooped up the afghans she kept on the couch all winter.

The world was silent and frozen. No moon, no stars. Their headlights swept eerily across the trees as they turned onto the parkway around the lake. They'd almost gone full circle, when they spotted him, doing slow-motion jumping jacks on the stage of the bandstand. Wallowing through the snowdrifts, they struggled to the rescue. When they got there, Wes' gaze was vacant, and his skin was bright red.

"Come on, pal," Phil said. "I've got our car."

Wes just kept jumping. It wasn't until Barbara threw an afghan over his shoulders that he stopped. Half-carrying him and half-dragging him, they loaded Wes into the back seat of the car. Barbara climbed in alongside, putting an arm around his shoulders. Phil revved up the heat and, within ten minutes, they were at the hospital's emergency room.

About three hours later, a doctor came out and asked who brought in the midnight jogger. "We did," Phil said. "We're neighbors."

"He's lucky you found him," the doctor said. "If you hadn't, he might have lost some fingers and some toes.

Maybe a whole lot more. People don't respect the cold. It can be a killer, even when it's not below zero."

Phil and Barbara got home around eight that morning. "I'm thinking of going back to bed for a little snooze," Barbara said.

"Not me," Phil told her. "I'm wide awake. How about I scramble up some eggs and fry some bacon?"

After breakfast, Phil got busy around the house. He replaced a washer in the bathroom sink, and painted a strip of baseboard in the kitchen. That afternoon he researched insomnia on the Internet, and learned that sometimes staying awake for twenty-four hours will reset your biological clock. To that end, they watched DVDs of old British comedies until well after midnight, when they finally snuggled into bed.

Phil slept straight through that night. And Barbara, as she drifted off, fantasized about being naked in a sleeping bag with Wes Larkin.

Janice Larson Braun – Poetry
## Two Parts of the Whole

It was meteoric
The way they came together—
All heat and light—
Impossible not to gaze on
In wonder
And amazement.

And then
They crumbled into pieces
And burned out,
Leaving nothing but ash
As a reminder,
A memory
Of loss.

Marg Walker – Poetry
Sharon Harris – Editor's Choice

# This New Arrangement

The flowers on your desk are not from me.
Pausing at your door I see someone's
jacket hooked on the ladder-back chair.

Things come into this house
I know nothing about. I know
the squeak of the basement stair.
The contour of your Saturdays. Where
the pots are kept, waiting for summer
geraniums. I know how sunlight shifts
across each room, returning it
to shadow. What can be seen
looking out each window.

Looking in after months away,
I withhold my knock. I see
our kettle coming to boil
for tea in this chilled, uncertain
gloom, a new arrangement
on the coffee table, your heel
as you leave the room.

Beth Spencer – Poetry

## Explanation for a Missing Lover

We were shredded in the beak of time.
Lost gamble, we are deleted chance.
Mere echoes, faint as deer hooves now.

Unraveled, we were tempests but
the weatherman was wrong again;
we blistered in too hot a sun.

The softest vowels, our carried cargo,
washed over all the words we cut from metal,
but still the edges burned.

Brief ode, bright poem, we melded
until time tore a ragged rift between us,
and that was all of it.

How remote, the mouth I wanted
How far away, the kisses rusting coldly
under the mutter of old stars.

Ryan M. Neely – Fiction

# The Zone

Paul Bettendorf stepped into the rain. Other theater-goers hunkered beneath sports coats and raced to the parking garage across the street. Paul tilted his head back and smiled.

"Come on, Paul. I don't want my hair to get mussed." This was Julia Brassard, Paul's best friend and his date for the evening. That's how Paul saw it. It was his thirtieth birthday and Julia said she'd celebrate any way he wanted. Dinner at Gary Danko's, *Chicago* at the Orpheum, and a quiet evening in the penthouse suite of the W Hotel (with two bedrooms in case Paul's luck wasn't as strong as he hoped).

He shook out his umbrella. As soon as it was overhead, Julia shot from the theater door. The weatherman had called for a sixty percent chance of rain. "Expect about two inches," he'd said.

Julia wrapped both arms around Paul and pressed herself into him. "Couldn't have found a smaller umbrella, I suppose."

Paul's grin widened. "Fits in my pocket." His blood quickened at her closeness. If he were a cartoon character with an angel and a devil riding each shoulder, the devil would have whispered, *Julia's gonna get more than two inches tonight.*

They rode the elevator to the thirty-first floor. Paul stood in the corner while Julia spun herself in circles, pantomiming one of the numbers from the play and laughing when she lost her balance. She reached out for Paul to steady herself, and his heart grew in his chest when she pressed her head against him.

When the elevator car reached the thirtieth floor, however, that swollen organ shriveled to the size of a raisin. A heavy bass vibrated through him. "Julia . . .?"

"Surprise!" she shouted, a too-wide grin plastered on her face. She leaned into him and pressed two puckered lips against his cheek. "Happy birthday!"

The doors slid open to reveal a crowd of three dozen or more of Julia's friends. They lounged on the sofa. They danced. They drank. They called to Julia and she flittered away from Paul to sandwich herself between two bodies gyrating to the music.

Paul's body deflated. He made his way to an empty armchair and sank into it. Despite his misery, he couldn't not smile at the joy plastered on Julia's face. He watched her for three hours, had four glasses of champagne and, at one o'clock, with the party still raging, made his way to bed.

He left the bedroom door open and stared out at the party and watched while guests trickled out the door, hoping that once they were alone, Julia would remember him.

She spent the early morning in conversation with a man Paul had never seen before, their heads huddled close together and, once the rest of the guests had gone, she led the man into the suite's other bedroom.

He may as well have been trying to sleep on the killing floor.

The following morning, Paul was awake and pulling on his pants when Julia crept into his room wearing only her underwear, her hair disheveled, and the slinky dress from the night before dangling between her fingertips. She smiled, "Good morning, handsome." She tiptoed to him and pressed her lips to his cheek. "Mind if I have a quick shower? I don't want what's-his-name to get the wrong idea."

She pushed closed the bedroom door and stripped down to nothing, unconcerned by Paul's wandering gaze. "He's a gallery owner," Julia said, gliding into the bathroom and turning on the water. "Thinks he can get me a show, maybe sell some of my work. It could be the break I've been waiting for."

A weight Paul had never before felt pressed his entire essence into a single point in the center of his chest. He stared at Julia's naked body and felt as though he was being drawn and quartered by his mutual desire to possess this creature and his need to rid himself of her. He sighed and said, "Have you ever wanted to be something so badly that it was killing you, but you knew no matter what you did it could never happen?"

She laughed at him. "What have I just been telling you? A real art gallery wants to—" She stopped when she looked at him crying. She crossed her arms over herself as though suddenly ashamed of being naked in front of him. "What's the matter, Paul? What did you want to be?"

His lips flattened. "Good enough for you."

Tim J. Brennan – Poetry

## Upon Learning the Next Clear Night is Tuesday

You come to me out of January
snow and when I ask for a touch,

you tell me all homes in Minnesota
have dandruff, and laugh

until my mouth shelters yours
against the heat of the fireplace.

In the deep evening of my fear, I tell you
my needs keep me grounded

until I turn to stroke the whiteness
from your hair,

promise to have you home
before dinner.

Marlys Guimaraes – Creative Nonfiction

# Weapon of Choice

The wind-knocked birch tree hangs on a barbed wire fence, catches in the crotch of a second basswood tree, which in turn leans into another tree, creating a cascade of danger to my husband who will slice the trees like sausages for heating our log home.

"I'll go into the woods with you today," I say, thinking I still like this guy and prefer having him around versus spending his life insurance. "Those trees are too dangerous and you shouldn't be out there alone."

I stuff my stretch pants inside socks to avoid ticks. They're my good pants but, what the heck, I'll just be standing there watching to make sure my dear husband doesn't get hurt.

"Maybe I should take a pen and paper along to do some writing while he works," I think, as I throw a purple stocking cap over my graying hair.

The red four-wheeler pulls up with two chainsaws in the trailer. I wonder about that, then remember Mike always takes two saws into the woods, in case one fails.

I'm pulling on brown chore gloves when Mike begins to show me the best way to measure lengths of wood sized to fit the woodstove.

"Why is he telling me this?" I wonder, swinging my legs onto the seat. I grip his jacket as we bounce over ruts, weeds, and rotted logs. When we arrive at the tangle of trees, Mike hands me a chainsaw.

I stare in horror.

He proceeds to explain how to use it. "Don't let the blade touch the ground. That dulls the chain. You can start by cutting off the small branches and piling them over here."

"You want ME to cut wood with a chainsaw?" I blurt out.

He smiles and nudges me with his words. "You can do it."

I stare down at the chainsaw. The chainsaw itself isn't intimidating. It's a small, battery-pack unit, easy to handle. Not like the large, heavy Husqvarna Mike was carrying.

"I suppose I could at least try it."

I hold the saw as far away from me as possible, push the start button, and touch the blade to a small branch on the humungous tree propped in front of me. It slices like a new razor through a whisker. Elated, I cut another. Soon branches are flying. I force myself to stop sawing long enough to place branches onto the slash pile. Then start the saw again, over and over until hours fly by.

When the battery pack dies and Mike's saw runs out of gas, we look with satisfaction at a trailer full of wood and a cleaned-up clearing. Rain threatens.

We pack up equipment. Before placing my chainsaw into the trailer, I hold it high above my head and proclaim, "I may not know how to shoot a gun or have a license to carry, but by golly, I have a chainsaw and I'm not afraid to use it."

Susan McMillan – Poetry
## And That's All

Your kiss stayed with me all day—
tamper-proof seal on the bottle of my self
—along with the ghost of your aftershave.

You backed out while, as a small kindness,
I leaned out from the mudroom, one finger
on the button to close the stall behind you.

Rear bumper of your old Dodge receded,
then rusted back wheel wells and bed
passed annoying point of sensor self-importance
where fights flash, door refuses to go down.

Halfway out you stopped, killed the engine,
wrested yourself from the driver's seat,
shook your head, muttered about
some thing or other forgotten.

Through dim-lit, oil-scented concrete storage
of mower, garden hoe, potting soil, cast iron
fake flowers and frogs who wait for spring,

you fought your way back to where I still stood
leaning perplexed in slow morning wit.
Without warning you pulled me tight,
pasted that kiss on my lips. And that's all.

Jim Jasken – Poetry – Honorable Mention

# Alzscape Reflection

My mind and I
Are playing hide and seek,
Your name concealed within my memory field.
I chase it first from when,
*Unbalanced,* we tipped the green canoe.

Remember that?
The time I lost my metal tackle box?
You laughed while I retrieved my floating lures.
We saved the stringer full of bass
That you had firmly fastened to the starboard rail.

Now your name takes flight
And hides behind
The pile of maple wood we cut and split
For that last beastly winter.

Damn!
I hate this game.
I filter through the alphabet and catch a glimpse.
It scampers now behind our wedding day
When we each vowed "I do,"
And you cried.

JJ Harrigan – Fiction

# Ready or Not

The old grandfather clock ticked softly. Roger hadn't woken to the sound in years, and he checked to see if he had left his hearing aids on before falling asleep. He hadn't. Not only could he hear the ticking, but he saw the clock numbers with vivid clarity. Some miracle had lifted the cloud from his glaucoma. With the ease of a teenager, he swung his legs out of the bed.

"Ah, you're awake," chirped a rotund old man. "Welcome, Roger."

"Who are you?"

"You've passed on. I'll be your guide until you're ready."

Roger remembered. The aches, the deafness, the falls, the impotence, and above all the loneliness as lifelong friends passed on. He felt none of that now.

"I died?"

"You passed on. You won't reach your final sleep until you say, 'I'm ready.'"

To double-check that his aches were gone, Roger bent over to touch his toes. He did a dozen push-ups. He used the heavy Bible on his wife's nightstand to do arm curls. He grinned at the rotund old man.

"Why would I be ready when I feel this good?"

"That's up to you."

"What's your name?"

"Whatever you call me."

"You're like that guy in *Wonderful Life*. I'll call you Clarence. What now, Clarence?"

"Anything you wish. Climb Pike's Peak. Talk with friends who haven't said 'I'm ready.' Visit anyone who ever lived. Or look in on any moment of your life."

Roger rubbed his chin.

"How about that time in high school when everybody cheered at my touchdown run?"

Presto! Roger was on the ground in the end zone, his uniform all muddy, and the football tucked safely under his arm. But very little noise came from the empty stands. Only three cheerleaders flashed their pom-poms. The tuba was gone from the band, and so was the bass drum and most of the trumpets.

"Where is everyone?"

"You're ninety years old, Roger. Your friends have passed on. And most of them were ready."

"Isn't there anybody I can talk with?"

Clarence handed him a printout. "Here are all those who've passed on but aren't yet ready."

Roger shook the papers. "This is all? Out of the billions of people who've died?"

"Most people become ready after they attend their funeral."

Roger scanned the list. "Adolph Hitler! Who would want to talk with him?"

Clarence shrugged, and Roger ran his fingers along the names in alphabetical order.

"Aha!" he pointed at the Ms. "This has always intrigued me. Michelangelo took years to carve that fucking statue of David. He never stopped. Never even took off his boots. They froze to his feet and peeled off the skin."

Presto! Roger stood in Florence next to the great sculptor who was hammering a chisel against the breathtaking marble statue.

"Get out of here," said Michelangelo.

"I'll be quiet," said Roger, leading Clarence to a corner. Soon, an aide brought the artist's lunch, a plate of bread and cheese.

"You'll get constipated eating that," said Roger. "Eat

those fruits and vegetables that Italy has in such abundance."

"He's not old enough to worry about constipation," said Clarence.

"That cheese will clog his arteries."

"I can't worry about that," said Michelangelo, studying the statue. He waved his hand. "I have to get this abdomen correct, and you're disturbing me. Get out of here. Guard!" he shouted.

"He wasn't much fun," said Roger as a guard escorted them out. "What now?"

"Many people like to visit their families of origin."

Presto! They were back in Roger's childhood living room. He paced on a soft shag carpet, while Clarence fiddled with the dials on a bulky phonograph. In front of the window stood a Christmas tree, with ornaments hanging from the green branches.

"Where are my parents?"

"They passed and were ready."

"They couldn't wait for me?"

"Everyone becomes ready in their own time."

"Take me back to my wife."

Presto! They were back in Roger's kitchen. His ninety-year-old widow wore a black dress and puttered with a salad she had insisted on making for the wake. With his new perfect vision, Roger recognized every ingredient in the salad. In his memory he saw her as a bride standing in a sexy piece of lingerie. He reached for her shoulders, but his hands passed through the mirage of her body.

"Are you ready?" asked Clarence.

"If it were just me, yes. But she'll be sad if I leave before she gets here. I'll wait."

James Bettendorf – Poetry

# The Key

The front door lock resists and the shed door
around back bucks, no luck there either.
It does not work in the garden gate, where
lilacs and lilies are highlights in spring
air, fragranced by purple blossoms. Yellow
iris prepares to announce summer's entrance.
I try several locks with no success, the china
cabinet where we keep saucers and cup sets,
the crystal and dried rose petals fallen
from a corsage—a long forgotten dance.
I move into the kitchen and the key fits
the kennel door where the eighteen-year-old
collie lies, his breath labored, the tumor
filling his lungs. We gently pick him up,
wrapped in his blanket, carry him
to the car for the last trip.

Andrew O'Kelley – Fiction

# Piano Lessons

He looped the chain around the hitch on his pickup and threaded the end through the legs of the piano. The castors screeched as he hit the throttle, scribing their route across the concrete. A crack in the floor was too wide and the piano was falling before he could stop.

The sound was musical: a thunderous, sustained chord marred only by the crunch of a tin watering can, now pinned beneath. He dragged the shuddering hulk out into the driveway. A faint chime resonated in the air. *Death throes*, thought Clark.

He'd watched a deer die once, on a hunting trip with his wife's brothers. *Just try to be normal,* Rhonda had pleaded. He'd tromped through the woods for hours in an oversized vest, toting an empty gun. No one had shown him how to load it.

Late in the morning the older brother shot a large buck. The two siblings handed their guns to Clark and grabbed the carcass, one of them noticing the animal was still alive.

"Clark, you want to put it out of its misery?" He tried to appear nonchalant, shouldering the brother's rifle. He closed his eyes and pulled the trigger. The bullet produced a spray of dirt near the deer's snout.

"One more shot, Clark. One more shot should finish it."

He ducked into the garage, returned with a sledgehammer and stood, the weight resting heavily on his shoe top. He kicked at the open lid. The white felt hammers arched in a fretful grin. He remembered sitting next to his mother as she tested an unsure voice, her confidence blooming with each chord until the two were swaying together and singing loudly, "Up, up and away, in my beautiful balloon," his little feet kicking a rhythm against the lower panel. He'd seen his mother in a new light that day.

A vicious blow split the front panel. A second broke the right front leg and sent several ivory keys skittering across the driveway. The piano wires twanged and thrummed, the soundboard groaning in protest. When the pieces were a manageable size, he tossed them into the bed of the truck.

Years earlier, before the layoff and the mounting bills, Clark and Rhonda had their own home. By the time his mother died, they'd had little choice but to move into her place. His wife no longer hid her disappointment. Yesterday, she'd decided the piano had to go.

Clark wiped his brow and turned with a start to find Rhonda watching. He staggered backwards. His shoulders ached, the sledge too heavy to lift. She stood in the yard, hands on her hips in a dirty bathrobe. He couldn't look at her face, the self-satisfied smirk, like he was burying his mistress. She spotted something in the debris and shuffled through the gate into the driveway, bending to tug at the spout of the watering can.

*One more swing,* thought Clark. *One more swing could finish this.*

Alice Marks – Poetry – Honorable Mention

# Vengeance of the Wind

Wind coming from cold
Something to hate
pressurized  vindictive
He should be able to see wind
It has weight
It has pressure
Born in an ice field
accelerated in a glacial tunnel
funneled through mountains
Blasts of wind
compressed  colder and colder
blowing snow sideways
Wind pumping blasts
rising howl each time
it accelerates

With each blast
he sways  tries to keep balance
driving nails into wood
Wood once alive
His own small punishment
A way to strike back at earth

Their marriage
a thing of pressure and weight
like the wind
Wind that will blow
until the earth is smooth
with nothing left in its path

He can see the end coming.

Sharon Harris – Poetry

# Keep Busy

when I'm not moving,
planning, doing,
crossing things off my list,

loneliness shoulders its way in
next to me and sits down—
a presence nearly as real
as the one
who used to be here.

New Arrangements

Norma Thorstad Knapp – Creative Nonfiction
Honorable Mention

## Nothing to Fight For

I came early to our cabin—a serene place—and sat quietly in my car. Later, strolling on the beach, I felt an edge of coolness in the air to imply the coming fall. The sun's rays shed a blue-white glimmer in the west, playing hide and seek in the trees behind. The lake was pale green shot with blue, cresting white when waves rolled in, then breaking on the sandy shore. In the water, my face reflected a heavy-laden Sally Fields look-a-like.

My husband arrived. His face was haggard, thin and papery around gold-speckled, gray eyes. He wore a wrinkled, plaid shirt with crisp sleeves that stuck out from his shoulders. White whiskers sprinkled like flour over his chin. We stood near the cabin, colorful leaves all around.

His sagging, slumped shoulders seemed to hold tales of buried burdens. His eyes darted, like he was trying to cover the secret life he led.

*Those lying eyes,* I thought. Eagles' lyrics jumped into my head:
*I thought by now you'd realize
there ain't no way to hide your lyin' eyes.*

A calm silence surrounded us, tranquil beyond belief. Smells of nutty wood smoke swept through the air. Nearby our black lab Shane panted.

Two items we'd left to deal with: our checkbook and keys to things we had agreed were his. After fourteen months of marriage counseling, our mouths were clamped tight shut. I handed him the checkbook. The sun now hung just above the horizon, streaking the sky with long shreds of purple and burnt-orange, fringing the woods behind the cabin in velvety shadow.

A metallic taste rose in my throat. My knees became boneless, ready any moment to let my lower legs telescope into my thighs.

We continued to stand on the grass where I'd often cooked summer meals for our grown children and grandchildren. There we'd feasted at the picnic table, draped with white linen and china.

The lake spread behind us. The water, where we'd made love dozens of times, shimmered like diamonds.

I dug in one pocket for a handful of keys—hard and cold to the touch. Keys to trucks, tool boxes, and places we had owned together. He took the offerings, eyes downcast, a ball of curly auburn-graying hair curving over his forehead.

A long silence stretched out. With nothing to say, nothing to fight for, I turned, thinking, *He values his marriage vows. He'll do the right thing.*

He'll say, "I'm sorry. Don't go. I'll get that help." But he made no call. No move. A cold, brisk wind blew in.

My crunching footsteps scattered leaves everywhere. Shane tagged behind me, whimpering. The iron-gray vault of sky tried its best to turn bright.

In the car, a serene quiet draped all around. It was not a meek quiet. Driving away, I felt the power in it.

Joni Norby – Poetry

## Ekphrastic: Alexander Gardner's Dunker Church

bodies stacked
like cordwood

ready to warm
the cottage-like church

sitting yards away
nestled near trees

with spirits peeking
out to see

saddled horses
heads hung low

near a horseless
two-wheeled wagon

a felled steed lying
dead nearby

while a pair of used
shoes sit waiting

Sue Bruns - Poetry

# Bad News

It hit me—
I don't know—not like any simile I've heard—
maybe like a cat that sits on your chest when you're asleep
and tries to suck out your breath.

That happened to me once. I woke in the guest room at my brother's house and a cat I'd only just met was on my chest—shifting its weight from one paw to another, leaning its cat head toward me, inhaling the breath I exhaled, staring into my eyes with its slitted cat eyes—cold as the steely marbles my brother used to have. I was paralyzed at first—not that familiar with cats, I wondered, is this a normal cat thing? A way they show you they like you? Stealing your breath? And for a moment, I was short of breath—the damned cat, I thought, had really sucked it out of me. But then I regained my composure, said *hello* to the cat. She shifted her front paws again—as if performing some feline version of CPR—lightly, rhythmically, alternating left and right on my chest. Is that a cat's way of pumping fresh air into me after sucking mine out? *I don't think that's appropriate,* I told the cat. She meowed a prolonged one-syllable response that glided from a middle C to about a G, I think, and when I pulled my arms out from under the covers to pet her, she sprang down from the bed and was out the door in a heartbeat—or maybe in the time of one intake of breath. I lay there, interrupted from a pleasant sleep, with the breath sucked out of me and no one to share that moment with.

That's kind of how the bad news hit me.

Dawn Loeffler – Poetry

## One Last Argument

She dropped her eyes to his keys
He picked up the hint
No brake lights
to illuminate the darkness
in their minds

She swept up glass
wiped the table
washed their plates

Her phone beeped
His apology
unanswered

Sirens were background music
as she flipped out the lights
Putting their saga
to bed

Marg Walker – Poetry – Honorable Mention

# Bright Room with Linoleum Floor, 1993

I am nearing the end of obedience

class with my intractable

black lab who pulls

like our marriage

first one way, then

the same way, but harder.

I have a foreboding

about the final test,

the stretched leash

taut with our straining.

Harrison Hurd – Creative Nonfiction
Honorable Mention Humor

# Girlfriend

I apologize for using the word "girlfriend." She's not a girl. She's a full-sized, fully-aged female, so I like to refer to her as "my person," which is a phrase I learned in Africa for the person that you're "most in love with" or "most attached to."

All right, so, the other night I get into bed with "my person." She's close up to me and I give her a modest nudge—otherwise known as "Swedish foreplay"—expecting her to immediately throw off the covers, strip down naked and begin fluffing up my tender areas with prodigious palpitations. "Palpitations" is where the word "pal" comes from. But palling around didn't happen, unless you call "palling around" the process of her removing my hands from her un-fluffed areas. It just wasn't the right night, er, month.

So, you're thinking these people obviously aren't together for sex. That would be correct. You only date for sex in your teens and twenties. By the thirties, you need to focus on your career. By forty the kids are teens and when one of the mates gets back from picking up the daughter from dance rehearsal, the other is asleep. Thoughts of sex start to pile up like collections of salt and pepper shakers.

When the fifties hit, it's survival time. One tries to pile up some cordwood of equity, a portfolio of red elm stock, a few oak bonds, maybe a pine rental house. The kids come over and drag off your best birch to pay off their college loans. At sixty you seek retirement counseling only to discover they've discontinued shock treatments at the local infirmary. Your mind drifts back to better times when all your friends were unsuckled hippies enflowering their minds on the milk of marijuana, but the milk went sour and now where are you?

I'll tell you where you are: You're in medical nightmare land. What's your cholesterol count? The good, the bad, or the ugly? Did the fiber pills work? Or did you need an enema? What's your PSA count? My new knee is better than yours. What? I couldn't hear that, you blind old stiff-ball. Pee into this bottle, even though you don't have a job. Is this the same vein as we used last week? Don't get your fingerprints on the X-ray that'll cause your blood pressure to rise higher than the EKG if you don't take fish oil every Saturday when you should be walking and socializing if you can just remember that at the desk on the right, I said, then your Medicare number possibly cancerous won't get you anything more than a lead condom for the rest of your life . . . and don't smoke.

Or you could just go out on the highway and lie down in the truck lane.

P.S. When I left a copy of this for my doctor, his nurse called to ask if I was suicidal. I replied, "Of course I am. It's winter and I'm in Minnesota."

Ryan M. Neely – Fiction

# Heart Day

A god stared back at me in the mirror. He curled fifty-fives until veins popped against his bulging biceps, but I didn't stare back. My eyes were locked on a spot over his shoulder at the blonde on the treadmill behind me. Mirrors don't lie. They only offer a reflection of the truth and this mirror's truth said a god was meant to be with a goddess.

This goddess—the blonde—I'd heard the girl at the counter call her Jill. Her body shone with a sheen of sweat and her hair was plastered to a face glowing red with exertion. We'd hovered around each other for a week but each time my mouth opened to speak, the best I could come up with was, "You need a spotter for that adduction work?" or "I've got a gym in my bedroom if you're ever looking for a *real* workout." Stupid, so I said nothing.

Today would be different. The god in the mirror told me so. When she finished her run and headed for the locker room, I dropped my dumbbells onto the rack and went to shower. I didn't want to lose her, didn't want her to finish before me and leave, so I rushed and was rewarded with a glob of shampoo in my eye. Showered and dressed, I grabbed my gym bag and exited the locker room in time to catch her ponytail bouncing through the door to the cafeteria.

Each seat was occupied, and it took a minute to spot Jill. She sat in the far corner nestled against a giant pane window. She'd brought a bag lunch and was setting its contents on the table—a two-top, and the chair opposite her was empty. Sweat beaded along my palms and the nylon straps of my bag slipped through my fingers. I lunged to keep it from crashing to the floor.

I grabbed a tray and slid it along the buffet counter. My fingers tapped against the metal railing. If there was such a thing as Indecision Flu, everyone in line must have had it. When I reached the omelet station, I rattled off my order in a single breath, and grabbed the omelet from the skillet before it was fully cooked and burned my fingertips in the process. I hefted my gym bag onto my shoulder and danced my way through the crowd to Jill's table.

She was dipping a fork into a plastic cup of salad dressing. I took a breath to calm myself and said, "Excuse me."

She started and looked up from her salad. Her eyes were the brown of forbidden chocolate and my mouth watered at the sight. "Yes?" she said. It was hard to tell if the word was a Siren's call daring me to brave her waters or a warning against icebergs floating at hidden depths.

My best smile plastered itself on my face. "It's pretty crowded," I said. "Do you mind if I sit here?"

She cast her gaze across the cafeteria before muttering, "I guess," and returning to her salad.

I slid my tray onto the table, dropped my bag to the floor, and lowered myself into the chair opposite. My omelet seemed meager compared to the mountain of salad before her. I reached down into my bag, now between my feet, and withdrew two five-pound dumbbells just large enough to disappear into my fists. On the ends of each dumbbell had been welded a different piece of flatware. From the one in my right fist projected a butter knife, from the other a fork.

A tinkling laugh floated to me from across the table. It was the kind of sound you'd expect to generate angel wings. When I glanced up, Jill held the back of her hand against her mouth, the skin around her eyes crinkled.

"What're those?" She laughed.

I glanced at my hands, self-consciousness blooming in my cheeks. "It's biceps and triceps today," I said. "I worked mass out there. Now it's time for endurance." I demonstrated by spearing a bite of omelet onto the fork and curling the weight up to my mouth.

Jill couldn't stop laughing, so I wiped the fork and rotated it in my fingers and handed it to her, dumbbell first. "Maybe you should try it." She pulled her hand away from her face, and I smiled at the way her nose crinkled to match her eyes when she took the proffered fork.

Ronald j Palmer – Poetry

## A Love Life

He waits but he knows
a stem without
a rose will not bloom.

## Tumbleweed

This morning as the dawn appeared
I saw a three-foot tumbleweed,
its thinnest branches covered
with a rime of morning frost
lodged between the markers in my garden.

It must have blown here in the night
bouncing all the way from North Dakota
spinning and turning on the wind
trailing winter in its wake and I
could only imagine what that was like.

Did it tumble its way along the arrowed
highways, avoiding passenger cars
and eighteen-wheelers, or did it stick to the fields
tuck in its many legs and roll across the empty plains
until it skittered across the river into Minnesota?

Like an exhausted messenger, sent to warn the king,
the tumbleweed just sat there in my frozen garden,
speechless, shivering at each gust of northern wind.
As sun melted morning frost, its limbs began to sparkle.
Only then did it tell me why it had come.

Deb Schlueter – Fiction

# The Final Pastry

"Twenty-three years," she whispered, a backpack digging painfully into her shoulders. "I gave you twenty-three years." A crazed giggle made her body shake as she stepped out of the shadows and looked across the dark street. A new blue sports car sat in front of a small, single-family house. "And you gave me what?"

Lauren McAllray crept across the street to peer into her boss's car. Ex-boss, now. The leather was glossy and new; a sheen of dust hadn't had time to form on the dashboard. She ran a finger over the smooth paint, whistling softly. "Fancy. This must have cost you a pretty penny."

In the back seat, the remains of a shopping trip. A bag of groceries, an empty bag from the local adult toy store, and a lost pair of fuzzy handcuffs.

Many times over the years, Lauren had contemplated being the person on the other side of those handcuffs. Her boss wasn't bad looking, and he was quite famous as a pastry chef. He had a huge home and flashy cars, and she'd never found someone to settle down with. Unfortunately, his personality was barely above bully.

Besides, she was his secretary. *Was*, being the key word.

"Twenty-three years working for your conceited, narcissistic self, smiling and pretending you were wonderful, and doing everything you asked," she said. "And what do I get to show for it?"

After a pause, she answered her own question. "Nothing." Her fingers curled into claws against the car. "Retirement—gone. Career—gone. Future—gone."

Setting her backpack near the car, she walked up the sidewalk to peer into a window of the house. It was dark inside. She scowled, hoping to have caught one last sight of her boss. Ex-boss.

Lauren could picture the owner of this slightly run-down home. A flouncy girl with no dreams beyond landing someone high on the pay scale, and dim enough to not know the man she'd welcomed into her house had the court breathing down his neck.

"What did they say brought you down?" she muttered as she headed back to the car. "Ponzi scheme? Gambling debts? Ludicrously expensive lifestyle?" She snorted and started to dig through her backpack. "And here you are, thinking you can get away with a new car like this."

She took a box out of her backpack, opening it to reveal a cake. It was nowhere near the quality her boss could've made—but then, she was the secretary, not the chef. She set it on the hood of the car, and pulled out two more boxes. Each contained smaller cakes, which she set in layers on the first to create a three-tiered confection.

The frosting was smeared and missing in spots, the top cake crumbled and lopsided. Dollops of frosting littered the car's paint.

"Gorgeous," Lauren murmured, setting a few candy flowers on top and picking up an icing tool. "I'd sell you for a hundred dollars. Then I could pay my rent."

Across the front of the cake, in loopy, icing letters, she wrote, *I know all your secrets.*

Stepping back, she pulled out the Polaroid camera she'd borrowed to snap a picture. "I really should keep this for the memoir." She watched it come into focus, her smile fading into a frown. "But I won't." She set the photo on the sidewalk leading up to the small home, a rock on top to keep it from blowing away before it was found.

Her backpack was much lighter now. She started down the street, fiddling with a tiny remote control.

She stopped a block away, looking up at the moon with a small smile on her face. "The cake was for me," she said. "But this is for everyone else whose lives you ruined." She pushed the button on the remote.

A block away, there was a blast of noise and a shock of bright light as the explosives inside the cake detonated. It wasn't nearly enough to destroy the car, but it certainly would put the expensive toy out of the picture. Alarms on the other cars blared into the quiet night, and shouts started to fill the street.

Lauren glanced over her shoulder and saw tiny flickering flames. Hopefully it was the glossy leather burning. And maybe those fuzzy handcuffs.

Kim A. Larson – Poetry
## Family Tradition

If you can drive a tractor
you're old enough to drink
beer, despite your young eight
years. You acquire the taste
sipping from your daddy's can,
sitting on his lap, barely out of
diapers, wearing a DEKALB® cap,
steering his John Deere.

You develop a tolerance while in
grade school, at family gatherings,
graduations, and wedding dances
where kegs flow freely and no one
cares what's sloshing in your red Solo
cup. Your family laughs while you
stagger about, your words slurring
as you carry on tradition.

Though the keg's missing at
your cousin's funeral, six-packs
and stronger tonics appear where
the family gathers afterward to mourn
his untimely death. No one mentions
his cirrhosis. Instead, you toast
the man who once favored beer
over taking his next breath.

Audrey Kletscher Helbling – Fiction – Honorable Mention

# Parting Shots

The salesman droned on and on about windows until Sarah couldn't listen any more. She kicked Al under the table, a not-so-subtle hint that he needed to get rid of this guy.

But Al ignored her and focused on the sheet of paper shoved in front of him. When her husband reached for the pen, Sarah kicked him again, this time harder. Startled by the pain, Al's eyes widened. He straightened in his chair, paused, blinked and dropped the pen.

"We'll have to think about this," Al said. "That's a lot of money, $11,000. I don't know."

Sarah felt the tenseness ease from her shoulders as she locked eyes with Al. Maybe, just maybe, he would stay strong.

"Tell you what, Mr. Swenson," the salesman said. "I'll knock ten percent off the price and throw in a free overnight stay at Pine Edge Lodge."

Sarah noted the rise of Al's right eyebrow, a sure sign he could be persuaded. They'd always wanted to stay at Pine Edge, but couldn't afford it. Surely Al would consider this a godsend.

She would have none of this. She remembered too well the time Al attended a home show and bought a $2,500 exterior steel door billed as Paul Bunyan strong by a persuasive pitch man. What did that mean anyway—Paul Bunyan strong? She canceled the order the next day despite Al's protests. She wasn't about to repeat that.

"Get out," she ordered the window salesman, not even attempting kindness. After two hours of listening to this man's pitch, Sarah's patience had long vanished. "You can take your overpriced windows and shove them. I don't need them. And I don't need a free anything. You think you can march in here and fast-talk us into spending money we don't have on this, this crap."

The salesman scrambled to gather his samples, to sweep papers into his satchel while Sarah glared, her words burning silence into the kitchen. She stood, stormed to the corner cupboard and pulled down a bottle of Jack Daniel's whiskey and two shot glasses. "Want one, Al?" she asked. He nodded and she poured.

Georgia A. Greeley – Creative Nonfiction

## Oh, the Farm

I know it's just a picture—I can't hear the grinder sharpening a blade—but I know that the wood-handled scythe and the wheel stone grinder that used to be powered by Grandpa's foot still live in the barn. The bales of hay are gone. The cows are gone. Even the chicken's ghosts are silent. The weathered boards and beams creak in the wind, a high-pitched noise, a stuttering squeak, like an abandoned child trying not to cry.

Michele Micklewright – Fiction
## Family Secret

My aunt died when my sister was in my mother's womb. Mom was on a ladder when the call came, painting the wall, remodeling their living room. I had just turned one, playing in the pen with Elsa, older by fourteen months, and Mom took us to our neighbors, ran to the hospital—the call startling her, making her run. Uncle Gus was in custody—in jail? But why? An investigation would have to be done, an aneurysm they said. It exploded and she lay there dead all night on the couch where he had hit her and she fell, he thinking she cried herself to sleep, but in the morning she did not rise and so my uncle tried to turn her over and she was stiff because she had died, had died a long time before her body stiffened from not moving. No charges were pressed—it would have happened anyway, they said—a clot and so my uncle was let out of jail and my sister was born that week, little Lil born the week my aunt died.

All I remember growing up was that my Uncle Gus was married to Aunt Alice and they had six children—our cousins and we loved to visit them in Beaver Bay and that's all I ever knew until my uncle and aunt divorced when I was in middle school and then Uncle Gus remarried and Mom spoke of his third marriage and then his fourth and I asked why—Why third? Why fourth? Then the story came out dark and quiet and almost in whispers. Then it was closed with—"now don't talk about this," so I didn't—only once in a while when siblings gathered to uncover family pains, to compare notes, to see what we had missed or forgotten because secrets were the rule; there was always a sense of whisper when the secrets and forgotten memories were told and for the moment we felt comforted as though the secrets could not hold us and for the moment we felt calmed, but then we left with the unspoken warning—"now don't talk about this," and so we didn't. Closing the memory sealed, entombed.

## Cindy Fox – Poetry
# Death of Local Icon

The grain elevator, the tallest building in town, was like a bank to farmers. Rusty gravity boxes, crowned high with bountiful harvests, dumped gold into the elevator's belly. Farmers left with a handsome check, thanks to their hard labors nurturing the land they loved. Despite the elevator's iconic appearance with the westerly sun shining in the background, its structure began to creak and groan, much like an old farmer. Once declared unsafe and not worth fixing after farmers were smacked in the head, it crumpled to its knees. Now sunflowers grow alongside the railroad tracks where it once regally stood, heads drooped like mourners at the gravesite.

Bernadette Hondl Thomasy – Poetry

# String Side Up

Alfalfa bales lumber on the clanking track overhead
Each one tips off, lands with a whump
Pounding the mosaic of bales on the hayloft floor
Bouncing dust mites up into sunlight slants

I roll a bale as quickly as I can, pick it up by the strings
Hand it to Dad, string side up
He grabs the twine strings with big sunburned hands
Packs the prickly hay rectangle into the perfect space

One after another, arms aching, sweat dripping
We roll, lift and stack a hundred bulky bales
String side up makes the hard work a little easier, Dad says
The clanking stops; we rest, drink cold water from a fruit jar

Down below, workers drive another load up to the conveyor
The parade of bales marches again
I grab a hay bale, string side up
Holding onto memories Dad and I make together

Marlene Mattila Stoehr – Poetry

## Bath Night at the Peterson's

Marks of the Old Country lay on the farm—
a small log barn with its straw-covered roof,
dried hay stacked on weathered wooden stakes,
small fields, tended with his sons.
Ed farmed as had his Finnish forefathers.

He was tall and gracefully curved,
like the wooden skis he carved;
his wife, Effie, round and jolly.
Many Saturday nights, Ed, my dad,
and the boys "took sauna" together.
Later, Effie and her daughter,
my mother and we girls bathed.

One wintry night, as hot rocks sizzled
and waves of welcoming heat enveloped us,
we kids, bare bodies billowing wisps of steam,
ran outside to roll in the newly fallen snow.
Our mothers sat upon two upturned washtubs.
And, just as Ed had imprinted
an old-world pattern upon their farm,
Effie stamped atop that galvanized washtub,
a heart-shaped indentation in the glistening snow.

Cheyenne Marco – Creative Nonfiction

# Soft Wood

White settlement of southwest Minnesota began in the mid-1800s. Settlers were not initially interested in the area that I called home. They opted, instead, for true Dakota Territory, pushing farther into the Coteau des Prairies. Just before the economic Panic of 1857 and the Spirit Lake Massacre of the same year, settlers moved eastward, claiming that corner of the state. They planted their stakes around the lakes: Okabena, Ocheda, East and West Graham, Indian, and Round.

Toward the northeast corner of Round Lake, there's a billboard next to a giant, aging oak. The Minnesota Historical Society calls it the Hurley Oak—named for the family on the east side of the lake and owners of Eastside Acres Campground. The sign declares that the tree was a land marker for early settlers. Personally, I would've used the lake as a landmark, but then again, I'm not known for my sense of direction and would've made for a boring pioneer. Nonetheless, the railroad eventually came through—slicing through Lake Park, Iowa, up to Worthington and over to South Dakota, leading to the founding of the City of Round Lake. No one needed trees any longer. At least, not for a sense of direction.

For more than 325 years, the Hurley Oak remained. Despite all her hardwood sisters falling to thunderstorms and age, she fought the elements and reigns just north of the boat landing. She bent under snow and shook in the rain. Sheltered Sisseton Sioux and Norwegians. Watched prairie schooners drift in and fish-n-ski boats sail out. Timed the waves for decades, learning every secret of the lake. Her life, lived in the shedding of leaves and dropping of acorns, condensed by time into rings. Whole worlds shrunk to lines deep beneath her bark.

If reincarnation is the true path of the soul, I hope to be reborn an acorn, dropped from the Hurley Oak. I pray I take root in the soils by the lake, to see what the next hundred years brings, to learn more from the teachings of time.

Peggy Trojan – Poetry

## Trail

Taking the short cut
through the back forty,
my eyes centered on a pair
of baby owls huddled at the base
of a tall poplar.
Their eyes were wide
and unblinking and they
did not move as they stared.
They pretended they
were not really there at all,
and I walked on,
pretending not to see them.

Shelley Getten – Poetry

# The Grass is Greener

cows lowered heads
between bottom strands
of barbed wire

bent front legs
to kneel in prayer
to the god of the other
side of the fence

their tongues stretched
and curled toward the grace
of green tendrils

as if they could be saved
by such decadence

Luke Anderson – Poetry

# Old Tucker

Old Tucker naps on my kitchen floor,
greyed nose resting on forepaws.
Somewhere show dogs pose,
sheep dogs nip, and sled dogs tug,
while Tucker lies on a braided rug.

Once he was a fine retriever.
Age has dulled canine instincts
and his urge to hunt is gone. Yet,
he knows my coming and leaving
and feels my joy and my grieving.

He struggles up on painful haunches
to look for me through milky eyes.
I pat his noble head and know,
we've grown old together and
performance no longer matters.

Tarah L. Wolff – Creative Nonfiction
# Hay Baling on September 2nd

A local attorney in town calls me from time to time when they need a second witness. It's generally for wills and the kind of thing you would expect. I was driving over there one morning, going through the radio stations and finally giving up in disgust when all they had on was the news. (I do not listen to the news anymore.)

I sat down in the office beside a little old lady while we waited for the other witness to show up.

She said, "I was thirteen when my father needed me to drive the tractor pulling the baler. I was so scared but the boy that was helping him, he was a Fitcher, you know, didn't show up that morning, I tell ya! So I had to do it!"

(This is my favorite part of this job.) I got us both a cup of coffee as she continued.

"So there we were, it was hot as the dickens, my father is out back and I'm driving as best as I can."

(I've moved a lot of hay myself and know exactly what that hot day smelled and felt like: Like Heaven if Heaven was unbearably itchy and sweaty.)

"And then there were all these cars driving by, we were out on the Ponsford Prairie, you know, and these people are waving and just going crazy!"

(Oh, my God, please tell me she didn't bale her dad! Oh no, please at least let him only lose a limb or something; it is WAY too early for this!)

"And you know what happened?"

I could only shake my head in response.

"My father came running around and told me to turn the tractor off so we could hear 'em!"

(Oh, thank God, her dad is alive!)

"One of those cars pulled over and we could just barely hear him!"

I asked her, "What did he say?"

"He said the war is over!" She slapped my leg. "I didn't have to bale anymore that day!"

Sue Kral – Poetry

# Contentment

In the warm earth of
the garden, two little hens
enjoy a dirt bath.

Jeanne Everhart – Creative Nonfiction

# Robot Cows

At first amazement fills my senses, seeing bovines accustomed to the routine of accepting the machine with no hesitation. Robot machines efficiently wash and grasp the cow's udder. My mind can hardly sort out the information being collected by the computer, as all the systems work together to do their job of collecting milk for a hungry world. The robot weighs the Holstein, records the amount of milk taken from the cow, and the time it took to extract. Is it any wonder that children think milk comes from white plastic bottles or those waxed cardboard containers at the supermarket?

They are no longer named Bessie, Ruby Girl, Clarabelle or Rosalie. They are black and white eating machines, numbered 64, 58, and 23. They are like robots standing in line to be milked by a robot that executes the mechanical task with perfection. The animals perform as thoughtless and unconcerned as the impersonal metal cups that grab their udders and drain them.

These cows never see a pasture, and they do not know the warm touch of a human. The cow does not feel a person she knows resting their forehead against her belly. She does not let down milk as a gift at the urging of warm hands. The sound of the barn should be the soothing rhythm of white liquid squirting into the milk pail. At least that is how the cow barn of my memory is. Their big brown moist eyes look at me as I look back, feel warm breath on my face and marvel at the gentle, giant heads.

Sadness creeps inside me, seeing beautiful little calves in a separate barn, stepping up to a machine to be fed.

Some newborns bawl for a mother, but they will not know her udder, and soon will not know why they call.

    I can no longer go to the pasture and call "Come boss" and herd the girls into the barn. While the adults milked, I brushed and braided memories into coarse cow tails. Milking was a family experience of talking in hushed voices in the warm barn sanctuary with sounds of milk filling buckets and cows chewing cuds. Smells, sounds and the scene became part of my being. I am dispirited, thinking of memories that my grandchildren will never share in the barn with my family. The human relationship to cows, pasture and milking is gone. The childhood farm I knew has given way to a digital, mechanical, computerized world that is foreign to me.

    Perhaps I still have a fragment of Swedish ancestry in my being that longs for the sound of *Kulning*, ancient Swedish herd calling. I wonder if today's generation will miss what they have never known. Perhaps they will know something is missing in their existence but, like the newborn calves, they too will accept and conform.

Kit Rohrbach – Poetry

# Secrets

Easy
to have a dumpster delivered,
to put everything in it:
clothes, dishes, paintings,
dining room table,
mahogany desk
with secret compartments
always empty,
even hidden drawers
could not be trusted.

Last to go were the photo albums
—that's where the secrets were,
around the eyes of the children,
their hands clenched tightly together,
their poses small and wary.

Easy
to walk away from the empty house,
to stretch unclenched hands,
to say done and gone and hallelujah
until the funeral director said
you must collect the ashes,
and there was one more box
to dispose of.

David Eric Northington – Poetry

## Moving Day

Sitting in a wheelchair
The old man sifts through
A cardboard box of
Debris and memories
Of a life lived and lost
Hanging on the wall
The portrait of his dead wife
Silently watches the old man
Deciding what to keep
What to throw away
Regret fills the small room

Mike Lein – Creative Nonfiction

# Someday

A few years ago, a friend took me to his family's vacant farm in far northern Minnesota. There wasn't any livestock roaming the overgrown pasture and only a crumbling foundation remained of the barn. But there were signs the farm had once been occupied by frugal Scandinavian farmers like the ones I grew up with over fifty years ago. Like the low head-smacking rafters in the upstairs bedrooms of the house and the outhouse, overlooking a pond, still usable even though the house had indoor plumbing. Why spend extra money for a high ceiling in a space only used for sleeping? Or demolish an outhouse that still worked fine and might be needed someday?

I walked into the cocklebur- and itchweed-infested grove of boxelder trees encircling the yard and found the open air junkyard I expected. Hulks of long dead farm equipment. Rolls of rusty twisted barbwire. Heaps of scrap parts from tractors and plows. Parting with metal was hard for these guys. A new machine might break down. Or maybe a hunk of rusting metal might be needed to mend a broken part or to practice welding skills. All this stuff might have a use—or be worth something—someday.

I do understand this train of thought. My wife says I have saved plenty of worthless junk myself. As usual, she's probably right. In my defense, there is at least one thing I have questioned saving, even as a kid, and not just some days.

Chores were an everyday fact of life back then and probably still for farm kids today. Holding slopping buckets of milk under calves' noses, trying to remember which of the pushy, bawling black and white horde had already drunk. Shoveling manure from calf pens and spreading fresh bales. Milking cows and driving tractors once you were old enough. These had a clear purpose, an outcome, and even were fun on some days.

But on a rainy day, a snowy day, a slow day, or as punishment for some misdeed, we had the worst of duties. Go to the musty dark back corner of the dirt-floored machine shed. Select a warped, paint-peeling, half-rotten board from a never shrinking pile. Pull the most obvious nails with an old claw hammer. Run the hammer up and down the board, listening and feeling for the scrape of the one last unseen nail that was always there. Stack the board in a corner. Pound the bent nails semi-flat while pounding and pinching fingers flat in the process. Drop the semi-straight nails into an old coffee can to be used somewhere, "good enough" for some mythical project someday.

The machine shed at my friend's farm was still standing. I unlatched the door and stepped inside. There they were, the fruit of the hard labor of many farm kids over many years. Shelves filled with faded coffee cans brimming with used rusty nails. Still waiting for "someday."

Luke Anderson – Poetry

# Corn Crib

Our corn crib sits beside a ripened field
where a combine roars and clatters past
in clouds of chaff swirling over
broken stalks and scattered husks.

Our crib once dried whole ears of corn.
Now we shell our corn in the field,
then dry and store until the time is right
to sell the golden kernels for top cash yield.

Today, the empty crib sags on weathered studs
while drying winds flow through its beveled slats.
It moans in mournful woodwind sharps and flats,
humming a dirge while it dries itself to death.

Kit Rohrbach – Poetry

# Why I Don't Wear Hearing Aids

Shadows of sounds
fray at the edges,
become unintentional.
*Couples make the best windmills.*

Amorphous echoes
rattle, reshape themselves
like drifts of windblown leaves.
*Evan's younger buffalo is back.*

Sense somersaults
with a playful tumble
into the slithery gap
between what you said
and what I heard you say.

There is only pure delight
when you lean close
for a confidential murmur.
*The lizard has lice.*

Jean Scoon – Fiction – Honorable Mention

# Moving On

"We never have to walk a step here if we don't want to," she said with a note of triumph in her voice.

Ben looked at the two elderly ladies sitting across from him in wheelchairs in the community room of Sacred Heart Nursing Home. The sisters whose farm he'd bought a few weeks ago.

He'd met Ione and Greta at the closing and had come to visit them now that they'd finished their move and had had a few weeks to settle in. On the drive over, he'd braced himself for the inevitable questions about the farmhouse and land. He dreaded having to tell them that everything had been torn down.

He and his wife, Ashley, were moving from St. Paul to Central Minnesota with their two small children and were putting up their dream house where Ione and Greta's farm had been.

When the Realtor had shown Ben the house and barn and a few smaller buildings, including a small stable and corral—they plowed with a horse, if you can believe it, the Realtor had said—he'd thought to himself how easily they'd come down, they were so dilapidated. He'd hardly been able to hide his surprise that anyone had been living in them recently.

The farmhouse had looked tidy enough inside, but was cramped and dark, with tarpaper repairs here and there. And no indoor plumbing. There was an outhouse in the back. He'd been flabbergasted. Who still used an outhouse in 1975?

The two women were smiling at him, obviously

expecting a response to their pleasure over the wheelchairs.

"Really?" he said, leaning forward. "Do you have trouble walking?"

"Oh no," Greta chimed in. "We walk kinda slow, what with arthritis and all, but there's nothing wrong with our legs. But why would we want to walk when someone will push us?"

They went on, now Greta, now Ione, interrupting each other in their enthusiasm to boast—that was the only word for it, Ben thought to himself—about their new home.

They were served three meals a day every day. There were snacks in between, too, if they wanted. They had a bathroom right off their shared bedroom. They each had their own bed.

They pointed out the television in another corner of the community room. It was on, and several old folks, some in wheelchairs, some on a sofa, were sitting around it, watching silently. The sisters told Ben they could watch TV anytime they wanted to.

They chatted on, while he listened, nodded and smiled. When it came time to go, he pushed each over to the circle around the TV and said goodbye. He glanced back on his way out of the room. They were already absorbed in the show.

While he retraced his steps down the hall to the lobby and out of the building, it hit him how foolish he'd been.

In his mind's eye, he saw the hillsides covered with scrub grass and low bushes and occasional stands of oak and pine. The gray heads of boulders broke through here and there, too big for the sisters to take out on their own and not important to him.

They'd lived more than seventy years on a rocky

piece of soil that had barely yielded a living. Neither had gone to school past eighth grade. Neither had married, and they had no other family and never enough cash to hire help.

They'd spent their lives walking behind a plow pulled by a horse. Picking rocks out of the fields. Getting up and going outside to look after their few cows and the horse whether it was twenty below and snowing, or ninety and sunny.

He drove down the long dirt road to where his new house was going up. He smiled, imagining the rocky hillsides dotted with the small herd of Shetland sheep he and Ashley planned to pasture for her weaving hobby. He could picture Matthew and Annie playing in the yard by the house.

But what had it looked like to the sisters? Neither had asked a single question about the farm. Anyone would think that moving to that nursing home had been the happiest day of their lives.

Angela Hunt – Poetry

## Arctic Exploration

As you slowly fell into slumber
You let go of one iceberg at a time
Allowing the cold hard to drift away
On the ocean of forgetfulness
Until all there was
Was grace.

Janice Larson Braun – Poetry

## Bound

The dog—
Seventy-five pounds
Of sinewy muscle and fuzzy hair—
Slithers into my lap
Belly up
Eyes gazing deeply
Into mine
In a bid for closeness
And a belly rub.
He plants one paw firmly
On my chest—
A lifeline
From his heart
To mine.

Cindy Fox – Fiction

# Quick Stop at Walmart

On my fourth lap around the Walmart parking lot, I spot them. A gray-haired couple loads their trunk with bags. I move into position and wait. I shouldn't do this but I've been in town so long I'm afraid my husband may be concerned about my whereabouts. Besides, I'm running low on fuel.

The gentleman, who looks like Archie Bunker, sees me waiting. I give him a take-your-time kind of wave and smile. He drops his chin like a bull ready to charge and snorts frosty plumes in the frigid air. As long as their car is there, it's *their* parking spot.

I lightly drum the steering wheel and in my rearview mirror see that a car now waits behind me. Won't be but a few seconds until I can pull into the spot. As soon as they pull out of the spot, I can park and we can all be on our merry way.

All right. Archie and Edith have their doors open. We're almost there. Dressed for the Iditarod, they flop into their seats and the car rocks and sways. The couple huffs and puffs as they struggle to arrange coats and legs and torsos. Oops. Mother must be sitting on the seat belt. Two cars behind me now.

Okay. We're buckled in ready for takeoff. He starts the car. But wait. Apparently, there's technical difficulty in the cockpit. Archie aborts the launch to rummage in the backseat. A third car now waits.

A fundamental rule of the universe plays out before me: As the line of cars behind you increases, the speed at which the people you wait for decreases in direct proportion. Should I move on? The guy behind me looks deranged with rage. But I can't leave. Not after all this time.

Apparently, Archie and his wife have passed away because I see no movement in the car. Just as I'm about to give up, their vehicle lurches backward. Then stops. Captain Bunker now inches his way out of the spot. Careful, careful. He moves with the care of one performing brain surgery. More cars line up in the next aisle over as they wait for us. I hate people who do what I'm doing. Damn! This parking space has turned me into someone I despise.

Finally, mercifully, the couple clears the spot. My eyes brim with tears—I've got a parking spot at Walmart! Of course, I'm not near the entrance but I can see the yellow starburst logo on the horizon. I park and bolt from the car like a rocket ship. Hiding my face behind my parka hood, I run alongside the parade of cars that waited behind me.

I am not here to shop but to pick up a prescription. Only one person ahead of me in the pharmacy line, I'm out of the store in ten minutes. Hallelujah!

I start the car and a yellow gas pump illuminates on the dashboard. I head straight to the gas station at the far end of the Walmart parking lot. Cheap gas. No surprise all the stalls are full, each with one car waiting. I debate if I should wait but when a car pulls away, I move into second position.

Ahead of me, Archie steps out of his car and a powerful jolt of déjà vu makes my hair stand on end. No! The dashboard alarm dings and the yellow gas pump now flashes—dire alerts that my gas tank is dangerously low. Thankfully, no cars wait behind me. At the moment I shift into reverse, Archie recognizes me. I appease his scowl with a neighborly one finger wave and zip towards the exit.

One block down, I pay 5¢ more per gallon at the Kwik Stop. A small price to pay at a gas station that lives up to its name and no one has to wait.

Meridel Kahl – Poetry

# Resurrection

As shards of sunlight pierce the cathedral dome
of red pines and poplars, your old Chesapeake,
Maggie, runs ahead of us on the dirt road through
the woods, her coat the color of fallen oak leaves,
her ears folded back, the hint of arthritis in her gait.
I ask, *Why are those trees orange? Why are they dying?*
You respond, *They're not dying, they're tamaracks* and
place a scoop of needles in my hand. As a breeze lifts them,
scatters them like hundreds of persimmon-colored feathers,
Maggie races back to us in a rush, touches your hand with
her nose before charging off again, her joy exploding through
the treetops. You continue, *They'll start all green again next
spring.* On this late October day that is all I need to know.

Kate Ritger – Poetry

# Garden Nocturne

I know what happens in the daylight,
planting, weeding, harvesting.
And I know who's here
from grade schoolers to college kids and retired folks,
an occasional bunny, neighborhood cat and ground squirrels.

But who's here when it's dark? And what are they up to?
Deer, coyotes, raccoons?
I see tracks and evidence of snacking in the peas.
Some say delinquents are stealing the melons;
they can have them if they have need.

I'm not going to heighten security;
I'm just curious.
Who brought the chicken bone to the west door last night?

Paisley Kauffmann – Fiction

# Absolutely Ordinary

She reduces caffeine and eliminates alcohol. With her morning toast, she swallows a chalky folic acid tablet to ensure precise prenatal neural tube development. Nine months later, the father stretches headphones over her pregnant belly, and says, "Studies show Mozart increases intelligence." Their unborn baby rolls and tumbles under her taut skin to the crescendos of piano concertos. Late into the night, they peruse baby books for the perfect name, and rising with the morning sun, the first pains of labor radiate. Opting for a natural childbirth, she travails through the relentless contractions complicated by delayed dilation. With a primal scream, the mother pushes their daughter into the world. They gaze down on their newborn with ten perfectly branched fingers and toes and choose Olivia, derived from the olive tree as a symbol of fruitfulness, beauty, and dignity.

For the entire first year, the mother breastfeeds and the father reads Tolstoy and Dostoyevsky over her shoulder. Forgoing a career, the mother stays home to provide a wide breadth of inspiring experiences and restrict television. The father works a second job and the mother scrapes and saves to send Olivia to a private immersion school built with red bricks and impressive endowments. Wearing a Tartan-plaid pleated skirt and starched white button-up, Olivia masters three languages, piano, and table etiquette. Her parents attend every conference and recital, congratulating her achievements and consoling her failures. Classmates are discreetly vetted and strategically placed, or occasionally misplaced, in her busy schedule. Puréed beets secretly spike spaghetti and spinach hides in sandwiches. Empty calories never cross the threshold of her lips.

    Olivia grows to an inch shy of her father with the vibrant smile of her mother. She surprises her parents with latent talents deviating from their consecrate list of desired attributes. Unlike her parents, she is spontaneous, laughing easily and abundantly. Her lust for adventure both pleases and frightens them. Congenial and pretty, Olivia is voted most likely to succeed and prom queen by her high school peers. Applying to a seemingly lofty college, she writes a compelling essay and is accepted. Her parents refinance their home to cover the seemingly limitless tuition. Olivia excels in college, achieving grades and academic accolades. The college counselor promises a bright and successful future. However, a boy with a sly smile and ponytail hired to maintain the verdant campus is drawn to her blue eyes and golden hair. With assiduous persistence, he charms her into dinner and a movie. The boy has dirt under his nails and drives a rusted truck, but he tenderly and carefully cultivates her. Without resistance, Olivia falls in love.

    Reluctantly, the parents welcome the boy with poor grammar, calloused hands, and steel-toed boots to their Thanksgiving table but forbid the relationship to continue. In an uncharacteristic display of shock and awe, Olivia slams her fists on the table and the door shut. The parents relent and invite the boy to Christmas.

    Months stretch into years and, one fateful blustery winter night, Olivia surprises them during dinner. Baring her left hand and a nervous smile, she reveals the diamond chip engagement ring. Her dream wedding, redolent with lilacs at sunset, is planned for early summer. With a heavy heart, the father walks his only daughter, fastened into white silk with pearl buttons, down the aisle and gives her away.

# New Arrangements

Home from the honeymoon, Olivia raises her water glass and announces her pregnancy. Her life bounds with intervals of joy and frustration of marriage and family life. Each baby hurries to become a toddler before the next baby is due. The blue-collared boy grows into a labor union man. Olivia works part-time to ameliorate a budget strained by four children with another on the way.

On the eve of their fortieth wedding anniversary, the grandparents impatiently wait for the arrival of their five grandchildren. The door opens with a harried rush of wind and snow. Olivia, zipped in a worn winter coat, carries the new baby in a cumbersome car seat. Her long, dull hair hangs from a knitted cap. Olivia grips the hand of a bundled girl with pink cheeks, and her husband leads a parade of three sulking boys complaining of the long, boring drive. The cacophony of effervescing voices infuses the old house with life. Snow-covered boots drip on the freshly polished wood floor.

The gray-haired grandmother gasps and covers her mouth.

"Darling?" The grandfather takes her hand. "What is it?"

"Ordinary," she says. "After all that, she's absolutely ordinary."

Marc Burgett – Poetry

## Grand Portage
### Northern Minnesota

I have portaged canoe and pack between lakes too numerous to count and hiked as many forest trails, but this trail excites. I am hiking *Le Grand Portage*, a nine-mile trail connecting Fort Charlotte, on the unnavigable Pigeon River, with Lake Superior. It's the same trail trod by *Les Voyageurs* two centuries ago. They carried their year's harvest of pelts—beaver, mink, otter—to merchants who had traveled from Detroit and Chicago to rendezvous with them and exchange goods.

>trappers bearing
>twice their weight in furs
>top hats for gentlemen

The day is overcast and humid, the air still, the trail slick from overnight rain. My eyes are on the ground, watching for roots and rocks that lurk to trip the careless hiker. Ahead of me, a shouted SHIT! followed by laughter tells me that my wife has fallen but is not hurt. I stop and look up. She sits in a puddle of fresh mud.

>marriage tale
>stumble rise
>go on

The trail descends. The forest drops away as we enter a lowland marsh. A boardwalk with a railing provides a spot to snack on granola bars, chocolate and apples. We guzzle our warm water. The still, humid air clings to us. My wife, not one to tarry, starts back. I linger in the moment. Not a sound. Not a movement.

>thunderous crash
>the forest loses
>a grand red pine

Cindy Fox – Fiction

# Monday Morning Coming Down

Orville rolls over and a broken bed spring pokes his back. He covers his eyes with his forearm. His flannel shirt, saturated with bar smoke, reminds him he sat on a barstool for the last two days. He stands and the room swirls. His head pounds like thunder. Mouth dry and tacky, he opens the refrigerator. Empty but for a bottle of beer. He debates if he should drink it. Today is a workday, but so what? He chugs the beer, swallowing his sour breath, and waits for the alcohol to erase his hunger, his pain, his life as a drifter. He's tired of people calling him a loser. Today things will change.

Outside, he slips his shotgun behind the truck seat with hopes of flushing up a grouse on his return trip home. Orville drives down the minimum maintenance road towards the Peterson farm where he works as a hired hand. Another day of slinging shit, milking cows, and feeding the damn things, so they can shit again. He doesn't remember the last time he bought groceries. The Petersons have been falling behind in their payments and he's the last one to get paid. Oppression of this lowly status courses through his veins.

Enraged by what he perceives to be injustice, he takes out his anger on everything around him. He kicks the chickens if they make a peep, pokes a pitchfork in the cow's flank if it won't keep its tail between its legs. Barn cats skitter when he picks up a broom to sweep the barn floor.

The missus rings the dinner bell. Lunchtime. He ambles up the hill to the old clapboard house feeling weak-kneed from hunger. The dog runs when he steps onto the porch. The screen door slams behind him with an angry snap. Orville's body odor greets Mrs. Peterson at the table, that old sweat smell that hibernates in clothes that are continuously worn without being washed. And something else. Alcohol. She knows he knows there's no drinking on the job. She wishes her husband was in from the fields. Why isn't he on time?

"Have a seat, Orville," she says, jumping when the cuckoo clock strikes the noon hour. "What can I get you to drink?"

He wants a beer, but says, "Milk is fine."

He mashes several boiled spuds on his plate, ladles hamburger gravy on top. Head over the dish, he shovels the simple yet satisfying meal into his mouth. The missus knows not to make small talk with him while he eats. Lunchtime is for eating. Nothing more. He wipes his plate with a slice of bread and downs his milk. Missus is a damn fine cook, but he will not thank her for the meal until he gets a paycheck. He eyes the Dairy Producer of the Year plaque mounted on the kitchen wall above kindergarten pictures of their young son and daughter. Would they have received this recognition if not for him? Probably not.

He stands up and asks, "Any chance I can get paid today?" His rheumy eyes sag like a bloodhound's.

"Money is tight around here lately, Orville," she says. "Maybe next week when we get the milk check."

"You said that last week!" he shouts.

"Okay! Okay!" she says, twisting a dishtowel. "Let me talk this over with Robert. He should be here any minute."

"I'll wait outside until he gets here."

Inside his rusty Ford pickup, Orville smokes a cigarette. The floor is littered with beer cans and twisted cigarette packages. He picks up a red shotgun shell from the refuse and rolls it in his fingers. His eyes move to the house, back to the shell, and back to the house. He drags deeply on his cigarette and flicks the butt out the window.

Through his rearview mirror, he sees Robert turn onto the gravel driveway. Sitting all high and mighty in an air-conditioned cab of his dual-wheel John Deere tractor, he drives past leaving him in a cloud of dust. Orville's anger simmers. Then boils. They got money for fancy machinery. Why is he always last?

He waits for Robert to enter the house, then loads the shotgun. As he opens the screen door and takes aim, he hears a school bus whine and shift gears and, from a distance, children's excited laughter, "Mommy and Daddy, guess what we did in school today?"

Scott Stewart – Poetry

# ... (for now)

Last night I
dreamt I lay down.
I lay down
with a plastic bag
over my head.

And the bag—
expanded and evaporated,
instead of
enshrouding my face.

I woke. Out of the dream,
sad. Still here ...

Georgia A. Greeley – Poetry

# First and Last

I wrap this child and remember.
This quilt would comfort
and still her cries—
somehow soften the whooping cough
croup and fever—
would be an imaginary room
for her dolls and toys,
would wrap her in safety when lonely,
and be her tent walls when she wanted to be alone,
not just warmth but a constant anchor in her life.
Now, as I wrap her still form,
and lower her into this coffin,
the folds hold her tightly,
a fervent substitute for my arms.

Marsh Muirhead – Poetry

# Pompeii

I was thinking about the racing lava
that stopped everyone in their tracks,
covering them in a last adrenaline rush—
heels catching fire.

How much better prepared were the
small animals now similarly fixed—
frogs and salamanders, turtles and toads,
as the arctic cold of our long winter
swept down from the north.

Outside this window, beneath
leafless trees they sleep, under rocks,
in mud hard as iron, through months
of winter nights at thirty below zero,
unaware of the resurrection to come.

Laura L. Hansen – Poetry

## Dog Years

The thinner you get, the more your thick double coat
falls away like end-of-season petals.

We can follow your trail through the house, find
your favorite napping spots by your cast-offs.

Your rich mane has unraveled to the thickness
of a worn-out scarf. Your shoulder blades

rise-up in a "v" like the spines of a broken umbrella.
The flounce of your Schipperke culottes

barely covers your bony hips. But here you are,
beside me, curled in a tight quiet ball,

throwing off heat like a great slumbering bear.
Your scaled-down body is warming one whole side

of the bed, and me, too. Yet another gift
of the fifteen years we've shared.

Now, I must find a way to give you what you
need next most. Old dog, do you need another day,

another month, or a brave goodbye? Dearest Jack,
I am not brave. I have been crying all day.

When you are gone, I will have to leave this place,
the house so full of the seeds of your final flowering.

New Arrangements

Marcia Neely – Creative Nonfiction

## A Boxelder Bug and a Fly

I first noticed her in late September. Another Charlotte. Just inside the frame of the kitchen window, she had created a beautiful web, positioning it so the midday sun could warm her small body. Perhaps as well, it would nurture her tender eggs when she perished.

Over the last several years, we'd had a series of Charlottes since my husband and I first discovered a barn spider in her web just outside the front door of our country home. We called her Charlotte. During a summer that had been almost devoid of mosquitoes, we fed her moths from time to time. We've done the same with subsequent generations. Each year, our Charlotte died in September or early October after leaving a nest of eggs.

Our new Charlotte, maybe Charlotte VIII, lived into the winter, supported by the warmth of our home. After noticing her, we fed her what we could find. Until the first serious frost in October, finding prey for her was easy. House flies and boxelder bugs were the bane of our existence then. When preparing dinner or getting ready to serve it, I sometimes swatted a dozen flies. Boxelder bugs crept on the floor, on the windowsill, and sometimes landed on the table. They hid in the window blind and left sticky yellow droppings on the blind and window.

By mid-December, however, I struggled to find a live fly or boxelder bug. I searched in the newer addition to our home, a room featuring ten windows. First, I found a rather slow-moving fly. *I must keep it alive until I get it into the web,* I thought. It flew out of my hand. I saw another one and gently pinched its wing, then cradled it between the palms

161

of my hands until I threw it into Charlotte's web. First it stilled itself, clearly recognizing its danger. But, within a few minutes, it started wiggling, trying to escape.

Charlotte sensed its movement, rode a strand of web to the fly, spun threads of webbing around it, and wrapped it like a mummy. A little later she injected the fly with a toxin that liquefied its body. Later, she had dinner. After that, I grabbed a boxelder bug, and threw it, too, into her web.

Charlotte had two meals that day. I knew that it might well be days until she ate again, but I thought she looked a little plumper than she had a day earlier and felt proud of the part I played.

Although I can't explain the priorities that allow me to throw flies and boxelder bugs into a spider's web, my rationale clearly has something to do with the story of *Charlotte's Web* by E. B. White, which stimulated my compassion for barn spiders.

Stories are powerful. Perhaps someday, a story about a boxelder bug will change my behavior.

Tenlee Lund – Creative Nonfiction – Honorable Mention

# In Memoriam

My husband's parents are buried in the state veterans' cemetery. We don't get there as often as we used to but we still visit to bring flowers and pay our respects. There's no need for the usual maintenance required at other graveyards because veterans' cemeteries are immaculate —mowed, trimmed, all the headstones uniform and in military-straight lines.

On one particular spring day, we were delivering an Easter lily, my mother-in-law's favorite. That's when we noticed the blanket spread by a nearby headstone. A young lady, probably in her mid-twenties, sat in the sunshine reading a book with a small dog at her side. They could have been in a park—except they weren't. They were communing with the dead soldier whose name was engraved on the tombstone.

As we drew near, she left. The diamond on her left hand flashed in the bright spring sunlight as she took the dog's leash and they walked away, leaving the blanket and book where they were. She would be back after we left, giving us our private space and retaining her own.

That was almost fifteen years ago. We've never seen her again. Over the years the number of headstones increased, bearing the names of aging veterans of World War II, Korea, and Vietnam. But I am drawn to that one tombstone with the word Iraq on it. A connection was made that spring afternoon between me and a soldier I never knew. At twenty-five his life ended, leaving a grieving wife or girlfriend to face whatever the future held alone.

As I mentioned, we don't get to the cemetery as often

as we once did. When we go, there are flowers and memorials at headstones throughout the grounds, but never at this one; no footprints in the snow, no indication that anyone has visited. Yet on every visit I still see her, with her dog and her blanket and her book, and I feel a wisp of her heartache. So I go over to the young soldier's tombstone and lay my hand on it, just to let him know that someone still remembers.

Lane Rosenthal – Poetry

# You

I hear your voice
in the movement of the air,
you sing in the whisper
of the trees.
Like the tide to the moon
we are connected
each to each
in ways felt not understood,
where feeling is understanding
and there are no words—
only our bodies synchronized
to a single breath.

Jan Chronister – Poetry

# Hunter

Pelicans glide just inside
crests of waves
bellies almost touching water.
Breakers curl and fall
with an almost human slap.

Midday they fly higher
tuck in wings
dive into depths the way
I want to meet death—
close to the edge,
swift hunter on the chase.

Marlys Guimaraes – Poetry

## Drapes

He's in there.
You know he's in there.
You can tell because the drapes are open.
You knock on the door.

His smile greets you.
Your return smile is genuine.
You take his vital signs, listen to his heart,
review his medications.

He tells you he feels pretty good,
but needs Tylenol every morning
for the shingles headache he's had
since the kidney transplant years ago.

You laugh together about the time the pharmacy
refilled Tylenol with Tylenol PM instead. How he
couldn't figure out his exhausted state
until you checked his medications.

Then you pack your stethoscope,
finish charting and say, "See you next week."
You lightly touch his aged shoulder
on the way out the door.

The day the drapes were drawn,
you knocked on the door.
You entered the silent room,
his breathless body on the kitchen floor.

Marsh Muirhead – Poetry

# Wind, Some Trees

She had flirted all week on radar—
a streak of yellow inside a hem of green,
a flash of red now and then
suggesting fire in the sky, hail,
familiar objects in flight.
But with coquettish insouciance
the reds faded to yellow, yellow
to green, cooler blues offering only
a distant rumble, a ripple of rain
until last night.
Dressed in her best cumulonimbus,
the city's sirens screaming,
she crashed through the back door
with an ax and half a maple tree,
buckets of ice and mix
for a party that went on and on
until sunrise revealed the wreckage
of another morning after.

Cathy Wood – Poetry

# October Day

It was in early October when we put Mom's ashes down
in the crockery bean pot she had chosen years before.
The kind of day to walk through the woods and watch the
        leaves fall.
Or float your canoe quietly down the river; then sit on the
        bank
with someone you love, watching the river go by.
The kind of day when you want to breathe in the sunshine
        and blue sky
and keep it forever; while every vivid leaf makes your heart
        ache for its beauty.
The kind of day Mom loved.

Kate Ritger – Creative Nonfiction
# Rolling in Soil

Sisters like to tell embarrassing stories when new boyfriends come around. Here's one in my sister's repertoire. I was still in diapers but I was definitely mobile, and my birthday is mid-May, so I was probably about two years old. I was playing outside in the yard while my mom tilled the garden. She remembers that the soil was soft and warm and the next thing she knew, I was naked and rolling in it!

I'm not embarrassed by the story anymore. In fact, I'm kind of proud that my relationship with soil started so instinctively and so young. What could be more wonderful than rolling in something that was warm and soft? It must have looked very inviting and welcoming to me. I wasn't worried about bugs or anything yucky; it just made sense to be in close relationship with the ground.

That soil of southeastern Sheboygan County, Wisconsin, was the first I knew. While I knew nothing of its nutrient content or pH, it was my home and my norm for the character of soil. Over time I've learned that there are more microbes in a teaspoon of soil than humans on the planet. I've learned that words like silty or loamy describe its texture and ability to hold moisture, and that working in the soil brings people together.

I remember very distinctly my first exposure to clay: a garden west of Charlottesville, Virginia, that abuts the Shenandoah National Forest. The soil was red and slick. When it was wet my feet felt like my tongue suctioning through a mouthful of peanut butter. I remained baffled by the color. I had seen Utah's arid landscape of red rocks so I couldn't imagine how things could grow in red soil. But the folks in Virginia definitely grew things—delicious vegetables and flowers, and meaningful friendships.

Now my norm is the dark, semi-sandy soil of Stearns County, Minnesota, where I manage a CSA farm for a group of Benedictine sisters. I know these three acres of soil better than any other place, anywhere. Carrots, for instance, do well in the sand. I know how quickly it will dry out after a rain and, even though it appears completely flat, I know the corner that doesn't dry out quite as fast. I know where to expect rocks and gophers and tracks of creatures from the woods. And while I haven't rolled naked in soil since that time as a toddler, I know the best spots to play tag with kids as the sun sets over the fields, have a conversation with an old friend in the shade, and have a potluck picnic with the garden crew.

Katie Gilbertson – Fiction – Honorable Mention Humor

# My Retirement Plan

The people inhabiting the apartments I manage would rather sit in the dark than change their own light bulb. They step over pop cans outside rather than pick them up. They curse when the grass is too long and rant when it's too short. They're mean to me.

After work I rush to my second job. I need two jobs to pay the bills.

My husband's been dead three years. Everyone went to him for help. Now they come to me. He made lots more money than I do and had no problem telling people "No."

So, I want to go to prison.

In prison I would get health care, wouldn't have to take out the garbage, go grocery shopping, cook, or clean the kitchen. I wouldn't have to deal with car trouble, shovel snow, or pay bills. No one will ask me for help because I won't be able to give it to them.

In prison I can earn college degrees for free, exercise and let someone else make the decisions. In prison my family won't expect Christmas presents or for me to pay their divorce lawyer or car insurance.

I will have to go through the court system but I will plead guilty and help speed it along.

But—what crime to commit? I don't want to hurt anyone and I'm not going to steal anything from people who haven't given up hope yet. Still, prison is the way to go.

The day I made my decision to go to prison, I stopped in to rob a convenience store. It was late and the store was empty except for the cashier and some guy by the coolers. Good, a witness! I confronted the clerk and said,

"Give me all the money."

He stared at me, confused. "There isn't any more money. I told him that was all I had."

Now I was confused. "Who?"

"Your friend over there," he said, pointing at the guy who was loading up on 3.2 beer.

Suddenly, about a half-dozen police cars squealed into the parking lot. This was easier than I thought! I turned to the door and smiled as four officers burst through the door. I held out my arms for the handcuffs but they rushed right by and wrestled the beer guy to the ground. The clerk and I were grabbed and pushed out the door. There, another officer hustled us around the corner of the building. "Get *down*!" he barked.

The clerk and I gingerly crouched on the broken glass stuck to the asphalt. He seemed nervous. "You with that guy or what?" he asked.

"No, I just wanted to get arrested so I can go to prison."

"You're not gonna go to prison for that. But hey, I've got some pot to sell. I don't want the cops to catch me with it, but if *you* have it . . ."

"Perfect!" I said. "Can I buy it? How much?"

"How much you got? I have half an ounce. Say three hundred?"

"What? In 1973 I could buy a whole ounce for fifteen dollars. I don't have that kind of money. I have seventy-three dollars."

An officer was approaching. "I'll tell you what," he said hastily, "just take it." He shoved a baggie in my pocket.

"Thank you." I patted his shoulder in gratitude. I got a little misty-eyed at his generosity. Now I could become a drug dealer! That would certainly put me in prison.

## New Arrangements

When the police questioned us, the clerk wasn't working with me at all. "The guy pointed a gun at me and took all the money. Then he went to get some beer and she came in just as you showed up."

The police were busily focused on the robbery. I hadn't really seen anything so they just took my information. I kept trying to work it into the conversation that I had illegal drugs, but the clerk was giving me worried looks thinking he was going to get into trouble. He had been kind to me so I got in my car and left.

I went home, dug out an old pipe of my grandpa's and stuffed it with weed. After two hours I was able to get off the couch. I got a really good night's sleep.

How does one become a drug dealer? I drove around the seedier parts of town looking for customers. No one would come near me. It must have been the minivan. No matter. After a few weeks, there wasn't any pot left.

Maybe I'll become a hooker.

Doris Lueth Stengel – Poetry

# Red Geraniums

Grandma always had geraniums
on the sill of her south window.
They flourished there.

I, her youngest grandchild,
often played with paper dolls
on her stiff horsehide sofa.

Evenings we played Rummy,
a two-person version.
It seems like I always won.
(I suspect hanky panky on her part!)

When I stayed overnight
I would follow very close
behind her flannel nightgown
as she carried the tall lamp
into the bedroom.

On Decoration Day
those red geraniums
were planted in a small cemetery
next to six of her seven children
who preceded her in death.

Red geraniums always
feel sad to me.

Donna Uphus – Creative Nonfiction

# Barbi

"Where the hell have you been? When Bill told me you were coming, I nearly died then and there! It's about time. A dying person doesn't have all day."

I hesitated in the doorway; she waved me in. "Well, don't just stand there, give me a proper hug."

I moved closer, leaning down to her. She was frail, but her arms encircled me like she was gathering life from my body to hers. She smelled of antiseptic. My stomach rose to my throat; I held my breath.

The room was dark except for the dim light from a small lamp beside her chair in the corner of the room. It was warm, too warm. I removed my jacket and sat down on the sofa. She looked as if she had something else to say, but she was silent. It was going to be a long night.

Barbi wore a floral robe, the bold, colorful print out of place in the dreary room. Nothing disguised her baldness. Her cheeks were hollow, her skin gray. An oxygen tube wound around her ears, clung to her nose, and ended in a heap on the floor beside her chair, the other end connected to a canister resting against the wall. It was her lifeline.

"Let's see what you brought." She reached for the meager gift I forgot I clutched in my hand, setting it on her bony lap. Reaching in, she took out the book. "Hmm, a book of prayers. You're gonna need this when I'm gone," she said with a devious smile. She caressed the cover before laying it on the table beside the chair. Peering into the bag a second time she said, "I smell a candle. I can't burn 'em because of the oxygen and the smell nauseates me." I took the bag from her lap.

She slumped farther into her chair, closing her eyes. I looked at the floor. After a long minute she said, "Well, come on. Tell me what's new. Cat got your tongue?"

She stared at me with those piercing eyes, so heavy with misery that is her disease. I didn't know how to talk to a dying person. I couldn't find any words.

"Well, talk to me, girl. I'm not dead yet!"

My throat felt tight. Finally I said, "Not much is new. The boys are helping their dad put up the second crop of hay and Lydia is taking a drama class in Glenwood this week. I drive her in the mornings."

"What about you, what's new with you? Have you started writing that book of yours?" she asked, clutching the robe to her chin.

"No book so far," I replied. "I've been doing the usual: gardening, milking the cows, running for swimming lessons, a little writing. You know—same old, same old."

She pushed herself back into a reclined position and closed her eyes. She quietly said, "That's what I wanted to hear. Nothing wrong with same old."

Richard Fenton Sederstrom – Poetry
## Devil's Kettle Eddies

After so long and in such longing

Francis Fenton stands at the brim and brew
of Devil's Kettle Falls and
in this spray and foam of dream

pours from a cloudy glass vial an ounce or two
of water from the river named for some tale of Francis'
craft and shady artifice, Fenton River.

(Connecticut, shall we guess, 1724.)

The water slips, drips into the fast sheen of the falls.
The falls remix Fenton River, drop by molecule
into the Brule River, and then

a vapor of nearly discrete particles
spread and flow under Lake Superior and into Wisconsin
and follow U.S. Route 2 to near Brule Lake and then, then

becomes a ghost of the vapor of the river itself and Francis
spread wide
to contract again into the original flow

but out of all control save Fenton's wyrd gesture
spread out and in and out and in, undulating
until nowhere is not this river, is not less than anywhere.

Laura L. Hansen – Creative Nonfiction

# Night Writing with Dog

*Hey, little man*, I tell the dog, *Mama has blanket needs, too*, as I try to slip my feet under his sixteen-pound body which is curled into a dark spiral of determination as tightly coiled as a snake sleeping in the grass, as self-protective as an armadillo who has balled himself up in his ironclad armor, and still I try to wiggle my way in to part his exaggerated weight from the yellow blessing of blanket and at last settle for the shared warmth of his back knowing I am weak to be controlled this way, that I will never know how to claim my space in the world with such calm dignity, without sigh or complaint.

New Arrangements

Niomi Rohn Phillips – Creative Nonfiction
Tarah L. Wolff – Editor's Choice

## Family Traditions
*Not Lefse or Kuchen but Tinobong*
*Kaua'i, Hawaii*

Pilar and Ciano Ruaboro's California son and daughter, their spouses, and children have come home to join their three island-siblings and aunts, uncles, and cousins for Christmas. Making *tinobong*, rice cake in bamboo, is a Filipino tradition, and Pilar wants her grandchildren to know about their heritage.

We're the only *haoles* (Caucasians) invited, though Pilar raises her eyebrows and whispers with a hint of disdain that some of the California grandchildren are *hapa* (half-Filipino, half-*haole*). (Like, *uffda, my Norwegian son married a German.*)

The day before, grandpa and uncles with sons and grandsons collected bamboo in the mountains. Their concession to modernity, a battery-powered sawzall instead of a hatchet to cut two-foot lengths. Back at the farm, Pilar and oldest daughter Fely picked and grated twenty coconuts.

When we arrive at 10:00 a.m., Fely is assembling ingredients on tables in the garage. We dump *mochiko* (rice flour) and ten pounds of sugar into a tub on the floor, add butter, coconut, coconut milk, and sweetened condensed milk. We take turns stirring the thick mixture with a paddle—arduous work. Fortunately, Fely's husband and son arrive and take over.

Granddaughters, ages five to fifteen, are absent. "Inside . . ." Pilar imitates texting. Auntie Fely finally summons them and puts them to work rolling banana leaves to cork the bamboo ends. Married grandkids arrive, get busy putting the batter into the hollow-stemmed bamboo.

The generational conversation is good-natured and

some not so good-natured.

"Too much sugar."

"Not enough sugar."

"Well, *you* have the recipe?"

"*You're* the expert."

Some irreverence for the process—"Why didn't we rent a big mixer?"

"Because that's not the old way."

"Because they didn't have mixers . . . and they baked it in bamboo because they didn't have foil pans."

Meanwhile the men are constructing a corrugated-tin, box-like grill about 20' by 3'—wide enough for the bamboo to bake on top of a metal screen.

Three hours later, the first batch is put on the fire, and we gather to watch it bake. One son wears leather gloves to turn the bamboo, two others moisten it with wet cloths. They shovel charred, red coals to keep the heat constant, sweating, downing a frequent Heineken as the afternoon goes on. We eat sushi, chicken wings, and won ton.

Like our July 4th tradition in Minnesota—family milling around all day, eating, drinking beer, watching the pig roast.

Aunties, nieces, nephews come and go. The granddaughters play kick ball, then hide-and-seek. Their bare-chested, college-aged cousins join them, do handstands and backward somersaults. After their performance, they come back to the grill and crack a Heineken. I could be in Minnesota with swaggering grandsons drinking beer around the campfire.

Pilar hugs me close. Puts her mouth to my ear. "The family . . . all together," she says. "Thanks be to God."

We are the *Kapuna Wahine* (grandmothers), and I know her joy-filled heart.

Kristin Laurel – Poetry

# The Sanctity of Light

Light levitates,
but never lingers.
I've seen it sprinkle
on frozen fields of snow,
watched it flicker and fade
on a puddle or wave
before it goes.
Light on water is a mirror,
the retina of a dream.

I've gazed into the dying eye,
watched it startle, blaze,
in that moment
before pupils fix and glaze
as death darkens a room
without touching a switch.
I've felt the wick from within
spread from candle to candle,
stranger to familiar stranger,
in a lit-up room.

Sharon Chmielarz – Poetry

# What She Loves

A charcoal gray cloud-band
ringing the horizon, advancing . . .

its companion, the lighter gray cloud-cover
roofing the neighborhood . . .

wind in snow. A wild baker
going crazy in the flour,

a promise for more. Light and fluffy.
She loves being old enough to read

this weather, how it makes time
for seclusion. Solitary in winter

is even social. Makes sense. Compare
its aloneness to a spring evening's burn:

There goes Rachel driving by with her
boyfriend in his car, waving. "Hi! Bye!"

In winter warmth may come from two
hands cradling the cover of a good book.

"The talking stick is a Native American tradition used to facilitate an orderly discussion. The stick is made of wood, decorated with feathers or fur, beads or paint, or a combination of all. Usually speakers are arranged in a talking circle and the stick is passed from hand to hand as the discussion progresses. It encourages all to speak and allows each person to speak without interruption. The talking stick brings all natural elements together to guide and direct the talking circle." —Anne Dunn

This year, we received over 380 submissions from 160 writers. From these, the Editorial Board selected 84 poems, 25 creative nonfiction, and 23 fiction from 94 writers for inclusion in this volume.

Please submit again!

www.thetalkingstick.com
www.jackpinewriters.com

# Contributors

*Without the following contributors, this Talking Stick would not have been possible. Thank you to everyone!*

### Benefactors
Jim Bottrell (in memory of Louise)
Marlys Guimaraes
Sonja Kosler
Joni Norby
Edis Risser
Harlan and Marlene Stoehr
Marilyn D. Wolff

### Special Friends/Single
Mike Lein
Margaret M. Marty

### Good Friends/Couple
Joe and Janice Braun

### Friends/Couple
Bonnie West/Fredrick Hedling

### Good Friends/Single
Sue Bruns
Dan McKay
Susan McMillan
Alan Perry
Peggy Trojan
Elizabeth Weir

### Friends/Single
Jennne Emrich
Ronald j. Palmer
Susan Niemela Vollmer

# Author List

Luke Anderson
Lina Belar
James Bettendorf
Nicole Borg
Janice Larson Braun
Tim J. Brennan
Sue Bruns
Marc Burgett
Julie Chattopadhyay
Sharon Chmielarz
Jan Chronister
Chet Corey
Frances Ann Crowley
Norita Dittberner-Jax
Charmaine Pappas Donovan
Neil Dyer
Larry Ellingson
Jeanne Emrich
Jeanne Everhart
Edis Flowerday
Cindy Fox
Shelley Getten
Katie Gilbertson
Georgia A. Greeley
Marlys Guimaraes
Carla Hagen
Laura L. Hansen
JJ Harrigan
Sharon Harris
Audrey Kletscher Helbling
Jennifer Hernandez
John Herold
Dennis Herschbach
Angela Hunt
Harrison Hurd
Jim Jasken
Christina Joyce
Meridel Kahl
James Robert Kane
Paisley Kauffmann
Vicky A. King
Norma Thorstad Knapp
Sue Kral
Kim A. Larson
Kristin Laurel
Mike Lein
Dawn Loeffler
Tenlee Lund
J. Mackenzie
Cheyenne Marco
Alice Marks
Margaret M. Marty
Michael McCormick
Susan McMillan
Michele Micklewright
Michael Kiesow Moore
Marsh Muirhead
Marcia Neely
Ryan M. Neely
L. E. Newsom
Joni Norby
David Eric Northington
Vincent O'Connor
Andrew O'Kelley

# Author List

Ronald J. Palmer
Yvonne Pearson
Susan Perala-Dewey
Niomi Rohn Phillips
Deborah Rasmussen
Kate Ritger
Kit Rohrbach
Lane Rosenthal
Joy Saethre
Deb Schlueter
Jean Scoon
Richard Fenton Sederstrom
Stephen Sinicrope
Beth Spencer
Peter Stein

Doris Lueth Stengel
Scott Stewart
Marlene Mattila Stoehr
Bernadette Hondl Thomasy
Peggy Trojan
Donna Uphus
Beth L. Voigt
Susan Niemela Vollmer
Marg Walker
Elizabeth Weir
Ben Westlie
Cheryl Weibye Wilke
Tarah L. Wolff
Cathy Wood

www.ingramcontent.com/pod-product-compliance
Lightning Source LLC
Chambersburg PA
CBHW060748050426
42449CB00008B/1320